BRICK BY BRICK
SPACE

WARREN ELSMORE

BRICK BY BRICK
SPACE

WARREN ELSMORE

WeldonOwen
PUBLISHING

WeldonOwen
PUBLISHING

First published in Great Britain in 2016 by Weldon Owen,
an imprint of the Bonnier Publishing Group.

King's Road Publishing
3.08 The Plaza, 535 King's Road
Chelsea, London, SW10 0SZ

© 2016 Weldon Owen Ltd. All rights reserved.

www.weldonowen.co.uk
www.bonnierpublishing.co.uk

Editorial: Fay Evans, Hazel Eriksson
Design: Gareth Butterworth,
Kate Haynes, Emma Vince
Publisher: Donna Gregory

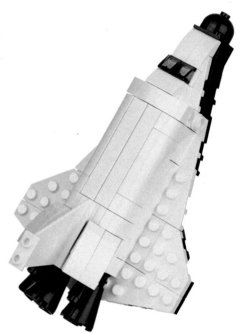

ISBN: 978-1-7834-2281-4

First Edition

10 9 8 7 6 5 4 3 2 1

Printed in China

CONTENTS

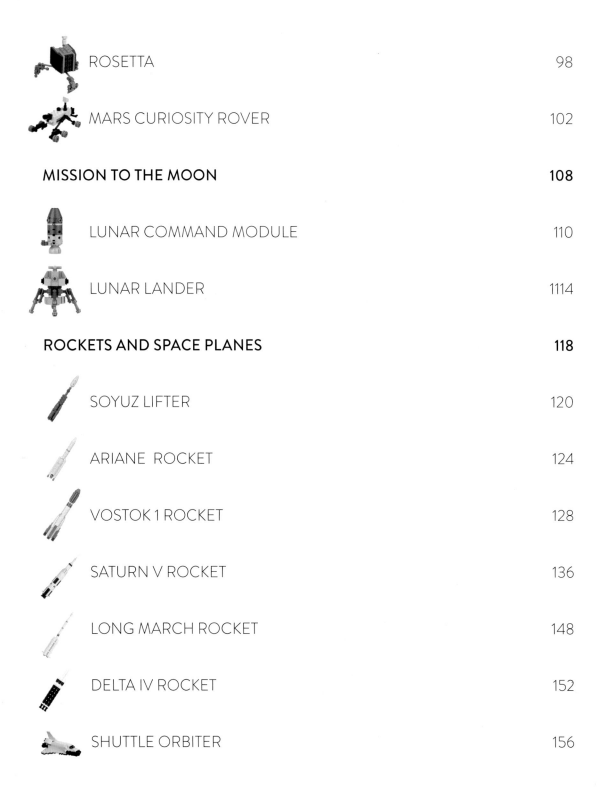

INTRODUCTION

WELCOME TO *BRICK BY BRICK SPACE*

Space shuttle Discovery heads to the International Space station in 2006.

There is something very special about space travel. Whether it is the danger of manned exploration or the technological challenges of the journey, people have been thinking about space travel for centuries. LEGOland Space® was also one of the very first themes to introduce the Minifigure® too, proving that space travel is popular even outside of the human race!

When we started with *Brick by Brick Space*, we decided to take a look at the whole Solar System. Not just the rockets that man has used to get into space, but also the space stations, the landers, specialist satellites and the many probes that we have sent out. When we'd decided on that list, it set us thinking. What about all of the planets that we've sent these probes to? Should we create destinations for our explorers?

It was a pretty simple decision in the end – we would create all of the planets in the Solar System and also Earth's moon – the only other planetary body that humans have ever set foot on. So the Mars Rover could "travel" to Mars, the Lunar Lander to the Moon and even Voyager II could travel to Jupiter. To fit all of the planets

Humans have always been interested in space. From Galileo's first telescopic observations of the night sky in 1610, to the Apollo missions to the moon and looking to the future of space travel, we are captivated.

A brick astronaut out on a space walk.

in though, there were two concessions that we had to make. Firstly, our planets are not all to the same scale! The difference in size between the Sun and the Moon is enormous. Over 400 times the size of the Moon, if we had created these two planets to the same scale, the model of the Sun would be 2 metres across!

This brings us to the second concession we had to make. As LEGO® models become bigger and bigger, the instructions needed to create them become even more vast! Making a model just twice as big can mean eight times as many pieces – especially when it's a complicated model expanding in width, depth, and height! It's just not been possible to fit instructions for all the planets into the book without removing all the

spacecraft (and even then it would be a tight fit!) so instead I've included instructions for the most well known of all the planets – Earth – and a few pointers to the others.

I do hope you enjoy reading *Brick by Brick Space* as much as we've enjoyed building the models and hopefully you'll learn something new too. One of the exciting things about space exploration is just that – we're still exploring, finding new things and new ways to study the universe. And what better way to study something than to build your own LEGO® model of it?

BRICK BASICS

The most basic building elements are the brick and the plate, shown right, which come in many sizes, but there are a wide variety of LEGO® pieces that will come in handy to build the spacecraft in this book. Some of our favourites are listed below – keep lots of these handy!

Brick, 2 x 2

Plate, 2 x 2

Brick, Round 1 x 1 Open Stud

Brick, Cone 4 x 4 x 2 with Axle Hole

Bar Holder with Clip

Brick, Round 2 x 2 with Grille and Axle Hole

Brick, Round 4 x 4 with 4 Side Pin Holes and Centre Axle Hole

Brick, Round 2 x 2 with Axle Hole

Brick, Modified 1 x 1 with Studs on 4 Sides

Bar 1L with Top Stud and 2 Side Studs

Bar 4L (Lightsaber Blade / Wand)

WHERE TO FIND YOUR BRICKS

Most of us have some LEGO® bricks tucked away somewhere, whether in the attic or under the spare bed and they're a great place to start to build some of the models in this book or your own space explorers! If you don't have any LEGO® around though (or the right piece!) then don't worry – it is possible to buy just the bricks you might need.

The first port of call is your local toy store and there are certain sets to look out for that will help you boost your LEGO® collection. The "LEGO® Classic" kits are full of useful bricks as well as a great selection of basic bricks and plates too. These are great to build almost anything.

If you need specific LEGO® pieces, it's best to turn to the Internet. www.LEGO.com has a great section called "Pick a Brick" at http://shop.lego.com/en-GB/Pick-A-Brick-ByTheme. Here you can choose which bricks you want by colour or type and order individual bricks. LEGO® don't list every single brick – but most of the bricks that we've used are listed here.

If you need a brick that LEGO® don't list on their website, perhaps an older or more rare brick then it's best to turn to some of the other websites available which sell LEGO® bricks. The oldest of which, with the largest selection is www.bricklink.com though there are also newer sites available like www.brickowl.com too. These websites are somewhat like "eBay for LEGO®"! Individual sellers from around the world list the bricks that they have for sale and you can select which ones to buy. Just be careful, it's addictive!

HOW TO USE THIS BOOK

The "Peices Required" lists have every type of brick (and how many) that you will need for each make.

Each of the projects in *Brick by Brick Space* is broken down by numbered steps, with the pieces you need for each step shown in a coloured box.

When the step is more complicated, it has been broken down into what we call a sub-step. This is where you will need to create a sub-build (or multiple sub-builds) to add onto what you have built so far. For example, you may have built the body of a rocket, and a sub-step will detail how to create a wing, which then needs to be attached. In this example, an icon will let you know if you need to make more than one wing.

TECHNIQUES

Building a brick sphere is actually quite hard. If you ever train to become a master builder at **LEGO**land®, it's one of the first tasks that they set you. So, recreating all the planets of the solar system in **LEGO**® poses a pretty unique challenge.

SPHERES

As you probably know, most LEGO® bricks are rectangular. There are some curved and domed bricks, but not that many. Unless the planet that we want to build is exactly the same size as an existing LEGO® part, recreating a sphere will need us to "cut some corners". The first way to do this is to consider the sphere in slices. Just like an apple – what would happen if we sliced the sphere into 10 even slices? Well, what we'd end up with would be (roughly) ten discs – all of different sizes. Now, making discs of LEGO® bricks isn't quite so hard. In fact, if you draw a circle on a piece of graph paper, you can see just how easy it is to make something that looks a bit like a circle – out of squares.

This is the first way of creating a sphere out of LEGO® and we call this a "studs up" build. Simply because all of the studs on the LEGO® pieces are facing the same way – up! This is a nice and easy way of creating sphere and it works

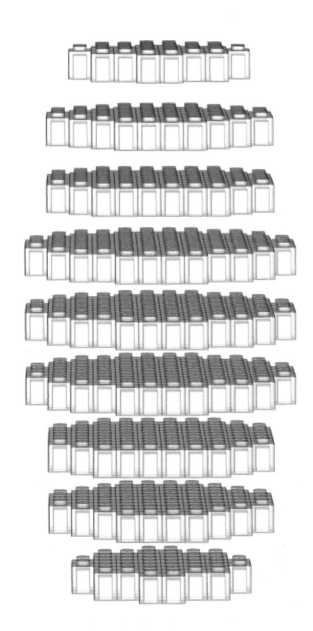

For simpler spheres, build and join separate discs to create a solid sphere.

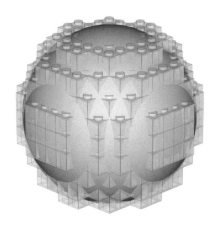

really well when each circle is large. Can you see how the middle slices of the sphere look rounder than the outer ones? This technique doesn't work very well for smaller spheres, though – they start to look blocky. And what if you want to add different colours to the sphere?

Thankfully, creating balls, domes, and other curved structures is something that LEGO® fans have been doing for a very long time – so a special technique has been developed to create smoother looking curves out of the same, rectangular bricks. This technique was developed by a LEGO® fan called Bruce Lowell. His technique uses not bricks, but plates. While a 1x1 plate is the same width and depth as a 1x1 brick, it's one third of the height. So, by using plates on their sides it's possible to create a sphere of the same size, but three times as detailed. This is how our Earth model is built.

The Earth model is constructed almost like a die. There are six sides to the Earth model, each one facing outwards in a slight curve. When these six are placed in the right configuration, each curve joins up to make a circle and the six sides become a sphere!

Working with plates on their sides gives us lots of detail, but it's very difficult indeed to build this sort of sphere just by looking at it – at least for me! Thankfully, another LEGO® fan builder called Bram Lambrecht has developed some software which allows these spheres to be generated automatically... nearly! It's possible using computer software to decide where the bricks are going be placed – but not how they connect together or what colour they should be. That is where your skill as a master builder comes in!

TECHNIQUES

If you want to get a spacecraft into space, the first hurdle is to clear the Earth's gravitational pull (that's the force that keeps all our feet on the ground). This is actually much easier said than done! To gain enough energy to break free from the Earth, it's necessary to travel at over 40,000 km/h (25,000 mph). That's the same as travelling from London to New York in eight minutes! Bar far the easiest way to obtain this speed (so far) is to put your spacecraft on a huge rocket and blast it into the sky. Rockets, though, are usually round – so how do we build those in LEGO® bricks?

ROCKETS

To make some of our rockets, building the shape in LEGO® pieces was pretty straightforward. There are a small selection of round LEGO® bricks and using these gave us the right shape to construct a rocket. However, a rocket isn't just a cylinder – it also has a selection of boosters, connectors, and payloads. So sometimes using round bricks isn't enough.

To recreate some of the more complicated shapes of the rockets, there are a selection of round-ish LEGO® pieces that can be used. In the body of the Ariane rocket, for instance, I've used an R2D2® piece! As well as being round, this piece has connections on either side for the two boosters.

The Shuttle Orbiter about to launch, depicted in LEGO® bricks!

The payload part of the Russian Vostok rocket posed a special challenge. We'd built the body four studs wide as this worked perfectly for that part of the rocket. The payload needed to be wider though. Six studs (the next round LEGO® piece) would be too much and the parts don't exist in that colour anyway. So we turned to a technique that is usually used to create columns. We've used a special 1x1 brick that has studs on each of the four sides. By stacking these on top of each other, but rotating them by 45 degrees, we can create an eight-sided column. Now it's possible to use these eight connection points to create something that is very close to a cylinder. In fact, with eight sides all pointing outwards, we can create a curve in the curved surface and make it even more realistic!

Take a look through the rocket builds and see if you can notice other parts that I've used in new ways. Not just round parts, but also radar dishes, legs, antennae and lots more. This is one of the really fun parts of building a LEGO® model – working out how to recreate a shape using only pieces that exist already!

The launch of the Atlas 5 rocket carrying NASA's Jupiter-bound space probe, Juno.

TECHNIQUES

It's possible that you might look at some of the spacecraft models in this book and think "that's not LEGO® – I can't see any of the studs!", well, whilst the studs might not show, I can assure you they are made from only LEGO® bricks. There is, however, a really good reason why you can't see many studs!

GREEBLING

In space there is no atmosphere – it's an almost total vacuum. Unlike on Earth, there isn't any air to fly through. This means that there is also no air resistance. If you look at aeroplanes or birds, you'll see that they are very streamlined. The smooth shapes help them move easily through the air without resistance. Take a look at WhiteKnightTwo and SpaceShipTwo – these planes operate at the edge of our atmosphere but still have to keep that streamlined shape.

Spacecraft destined for outer space don't have to worry about streamlining. There is no air to move through, so no air resistance. They also don't have to worry about gravity. On Earth, supports for wings, masts, or dishes have to be strong to make sure they don't fall over. In space, on the other hand, there's no need for this so supports can be much thinner and lighter.

The Space Shuttle, Endeavour and a 747 aircraft carrier.

These two factors combine to make spacecraft look very different to airplanes. Spacecraft have large solar cells to generate power and are bristling with sensors and communications equipment. This equipment doesn't need to be aerodynamic but is simply placed where it will work best. This has a big impact on how we build a LEGO® model. We've represented the solar cells with very smooth elements – tiles or sometimes flags. These parts are similar to the smooth surface of a solar panel.

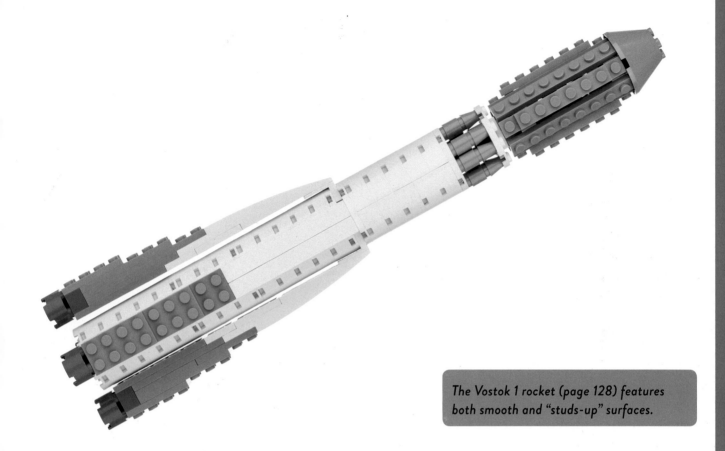

The Vostok 1 rocket (page 128) features both smooth and "studs-up" surfaces.

The bodies of our spacecraft, covered in sensors, are bristling in strange shapes. In the LEGO® fan world, this is called "greebling". Greebling is the process of covering a model in complex shapes, antennae, exhausts, in fact anything that isn't a smooth surface. If you take a close look at the satellites and spacecraft, you'll see a huge array of small LEGO® pieces being used to cover the surfaces. This is the easiest way to greeble a model. We've used lots of small pieces that attach onto studs – as well as many pieces that connect with bars or clips. These smaller pieces reflect the shapes of cameras, radio masts, and antennae.

If you want to build a spacecraft at home, have a think about where your spacecraft is going to fly. Is it going to work inside the atmosphere of a planet? In which case it will need to be smooth and curvaceous. If it's only going to explore space, you don't need to worry about the air and your spacecraft can be as greebled as you like. In fact, it might even be worth keeping a collection of those small "greebly" parts to hand. Just in case!

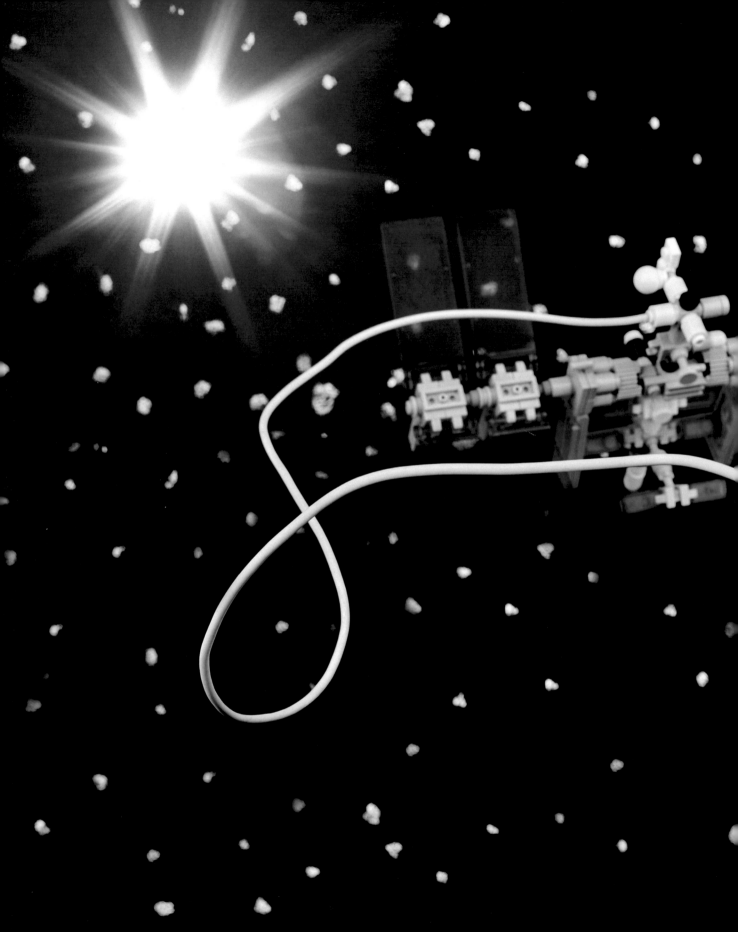

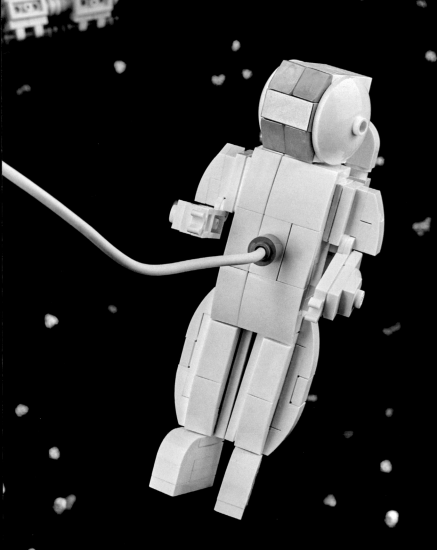

PROJECTS

THE SOLAR SYSTEM

The Solar System formed around 4.6 billion years ago from a giant cloud of gas and dust. At the centre of the Solar System is the yellow star that is our Sun. Closest to the Sun are the four terrestrial planets, while farther out are the four giant planets. These eight planets orbit the Sun.

The formation of the universe, also known as "The Big Bang Theory".

FORMATION OF THE SOLAR SYSTEM

The Solar System was formed when a cloud of dust and hydrogen and helium gases started to collapse in on itself. The collapse was possibly set off by the explosion of a nearby star. Gravity is the force that pulls all objects in the Universe toward each other. As gravity pulled the mass of gas and dust together, it started to spin. At the centre, where the mass was thickest, it grew hotter and hotter. Here a star was formed, our Sun. The rest of the material in the cloud began to clump together, forming the planets. Gravity keeps the planets spinning, or orbiting, around the Sun.

THE PLANETS

The four terrestrial planets are made of rock and metal. Terrestrial means "Earth-like". Starting with the closest to the Sun, the terrestrial planets are Mercury, Venus, Earth, and Mars.

Beyond the orbit of Mars is the Asteroid Belt. This is a ring of millions of rocky fragments, called asteroids. Asteroids in the belt hurtle around the Sun at an average speed of 25 km (15 miles) per second.

Beyond the Asteroid Belt are the giant planets, which are much larger than the rocky inner worlds. The largest of all, Jupiter, could contain all the other planets in the Solar System. None of the giant planets has a solid surface. Jupiter and Saturn are called the gas giants. They are made of the gases hydrogen and helium. Uranus and Neptune are the ice giants. They are made mostly of icy slushes of hydrogen and helium.

There are at least five dwarf planets in our Solar System. A dwarf planet is an object in orbit about the Sun that is massive enough for its own gravity to crush it into a roughly spherical, or ball-like, shape. However, its gravity is not strong enough to clear its orbit of other

Our solar system, in LEGO® bricks.

material, so its path is crossed by other planets or asteroids. From the smallest to largest, the known dwarf planets are: Ceres, Makemake, Haumea, Pluto, and Eris. Eris is 2,326 km (1,445 miles) across. Apart from Ceres, which is in the Asteroid Belt, all the dwarf planets are beyond the orbit of Neptune.

WHERE IS THE SOLAR SYSTEM?

The Solar System is in the Milky Way galaxy. Our home galaxy contains at least 200 billion stars and 100 billion planets. The galaxy is 100,000 light years across, and the Solar System is 25,000 light years from its centre. A light year is how far light travels in one year, around 9 trillion km (6 trillion miles).

The Milky Way is just one of 100 billion galaxies in the Universe. The Universe that we can see is 91 billion light years across. However, the Universe is growing and may actually be infinite, which means it goes on forever. The Universe began 13.8 billion years ago in a fireball of creation that scientists call the Big Bang.

SOLAR SYSTEM PROFILES

There are eight confirmed large planets and five dwarf planets in our Solar System. The closest planet to the Sun, Mercury, completes its journey around the star in 88 Earth days. The farthest planet, Neptune, orbits in 165 Earth years. In 2016, astronomers thought they might have found a ninth large planet, far beyond the orbit of Neptune, but its existence has not yet been confirmed.

THE SUN

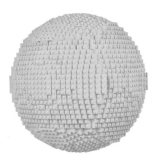

The planets of the Solar System are in orbit around the Sun, which is a 4.6-billion-year-old star. The Sun is a glowing ball of plasma. Plasma is what gas turns into when it is extremely hot. The temperature at the Sun's core is 15,500,000°C (28,000,000°F). The Sun's warmth and light makes life possible on Earth.

NAME: THE SUN

DIAMETER: 1,392,000 KM (865,000 MILES)

TYPE: YELLOW DWARF STAR

THE MOON

NAME: THE MOON

AVERAGE DISTANCE FROM EARTH: 384,400 KM (238,855 MILES)

DIAMETER: 3,476 KM (2,160 MILES)

TYPE: SATELLITE

The Moon is not considered to be a planet, because planets must be in orbit independently around the Sun. The Moon orbits the Earth once every 27.32 days. The dark patches we can see on the Moon, called "seas", were created when lava (molten rock) spread across the Moon's surface before hardening.

MERCURY

Mercury has a huge core of iron, surrounded by a thin, rocky crust. The closest planet to the Sun, Mercury also has the fastest orbit: it travels round the Sun in just 88 Earth days. Mercury's surface is marked by craters, where asteroids hurtled into the planet billions of years ago.

NAME: MERCURY

AVERAGE DISTANCE FROM THE SUN: 58 MILLION KM (36 MILLION MILES)

DIAMETER: 4,879 KM (3,032 MILES)

TYPE: TERRESTRIAL PLANET

VENUS

NAME: VENUS

AVERAGE DISTANCE FROM THE SUN: 108 MILLION KM (67 MILLION MILES)

DIAMETER: 12,104 KM (7,521 MILES)

TYPE: TERRESTRIAL PLANET

Although similar in size to Earth, Venus would be deadly to humans. The planet's atmosphere is made up almost entirely of carbon dioxide. This gas traps heat, making the temperature on Venus's surface 464°C (867°F), which is hot enough to melt tin. Thick clouds of sulfuric acid cloak the planet.

THE EARTH

Earth is the largest of the four terrestrial planets. Our planet is the only planet we know of that supports life. Life is possible on Earth because the temperature is right for liquid water. If it were colder, all water would freeze. If it were hotter, all water would evaporate. Water is where life began on Earth.

NAME: THE EARTH

AVERAGE DISTANCE FROM THE SUN: 150 MILLION KM (93 MILLION MILES)

DIAMETER: 12,756 KM (7,926 MILES)

TYPE: TERRESTRIAL PLANET

MARS

Mars is a lifeless, dusty planet, riddled with huge volcanoes and canyons. However, astronomers believe the surface of Mars might once have been covered by liquid water. Earth and Mars are the only terrestrial planets with satellites. The Martian moons are called Phobos and Deimos.

NAME: MARS

AVERAGE DISTANCE FROM THE SUN: 108 MILLION KM (67 MILLION MILES)

DIAMETER: 12,104 KM (7,521 MILES)

TYPE: TERRESTRIAL PLANET

JUPITER

NAME: JUPITER

AVERAGE DISTANCE FROM THE SUN: 779 MILLION KM (484 MILLION MILES)

DIAMETER: 142,984 KM (88,846 MILES)

TYPE: GAS GIANT PLANET

Jupiter is made mostly of the gases hydrogen and helium, under so much pressure they have become liquid. Immense storms swirl in Jupiter's atmosphere for years, or even centuries, at a time. Jupiter has 67 known satellites, including the largest moon in the Solar System, Ganymede, which has a diameter of 5,268 km (3,273 miles).

SATURN

All four of the giant planets have a ring system, but Saturn's is the brightest and largest. The rings are made of specks and chunks of ice and dust, spinning around the planet at a distance of up to 120,700 km (75,400 miles) from its equator. Saturn boasts 62 known satellites.

NAME: SATURN

AVERAGE DISTANCE FROM THE SUN: 1,434 MILLION KM (891 MILLION MILES)

DIAMETER: 120,536 KM (74,898 MILES)

TYPE: GAS GIANT PLANET

URANUS

Uranus orbits on its side. This extreme tilt may have been caused by a collision with another planet during the Solar System's formation. The planet's blue-green colour is caused by large amounts of the gas methane in its atmosphere. Methane absorbs red light, and reflects blue-green light. Uranus has 27 known satellites.

NAME: URANUS

AVERAGE DISTANCE FROM THE SUN: 2,873 MILLION KM (1,785 MILLION MILES)

DIAMETER: 51,118 KM (31,763 MILES)

TYPE: ICE GIANT PLANET

NEPTUNE

NAME: NEPTUNE

AVERAGE DISTANCE FROM THE SUN: 4,495 MILLION KM (2,793 MILLION MILES)

DIAMETER: 49,528 KM (30,775 MILES)

TYPE: ICE GIANT PLANET

On Neptune, the Sun is 900 times fainter than it is on Earth. This icy blue sphere is streaked by the white clouds of giant storms. The winds on Neptune are the fastest in the Solar System, reaching speeds of 670 metres per second (2,200 ft/s). Fourteen satellites of Neptune have been discovered so far.

PLUTO

Pluto was considered to be the ninth planet in our Solar System, until it was re-classified as a dwarf planet in 2006, because it is not large enough for its gravity to clear its orbit of other material. Pluto is made of ice and rock. It has five known satellites: Charon, Styx, Nix, Kerberos, and Hydra.

NAME: PLUTO

AVERAGE DISTANCE FROM THE SUN: 5,870 MILLION KM (3,670 MILLION MILES)

DIAMETER: 2,370 KM (1,473 MILES)

TYPE: DWARF PLANET

THE MOON

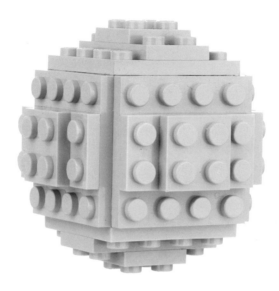

PIECES REQUIRED

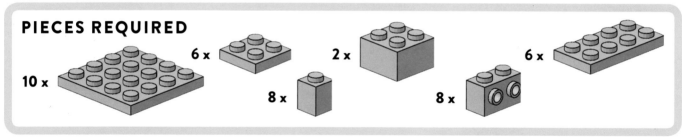

10 x   6 x   2 x   6 x

8 x   8 x

1

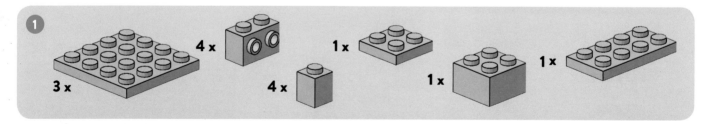

3 x   4 x   1 x   1 x   1 x

4 x

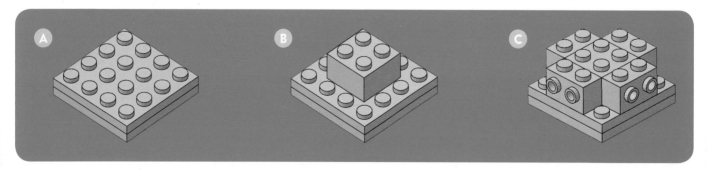

A   B   C

D   **E**   **F**

make
2

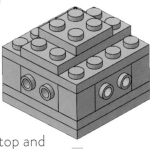

Hold the top and
bottom pieces
together until you
attach the sides.

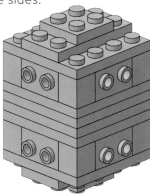

2

4 x

3

4 x

4 x

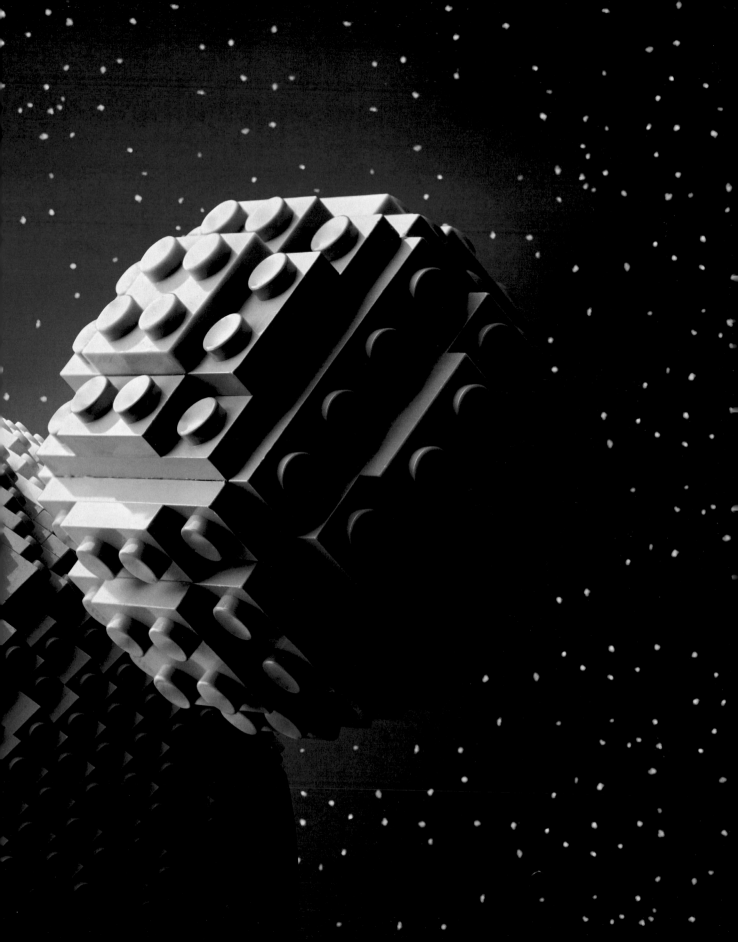

THE EARTH

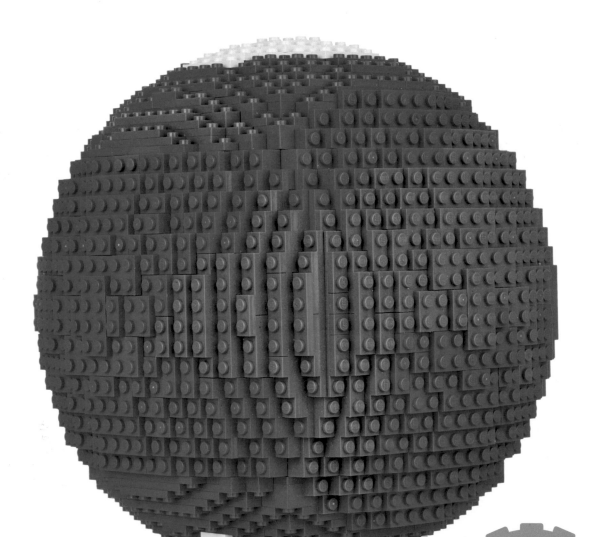

TIP:
Check pages
12–13 for an
introduction to
building spheres!

PART I

PIECES REQUIRED

4 x

2 x

1 x

1 x

2 x

2 x

2 x

1 x

2 x

9 x

12 x

2 x

2 x

2 x

2 x

2 x

2 x

8 x

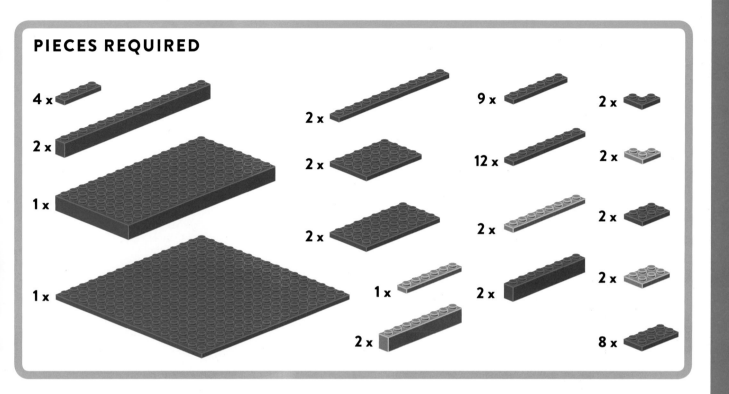

1

3

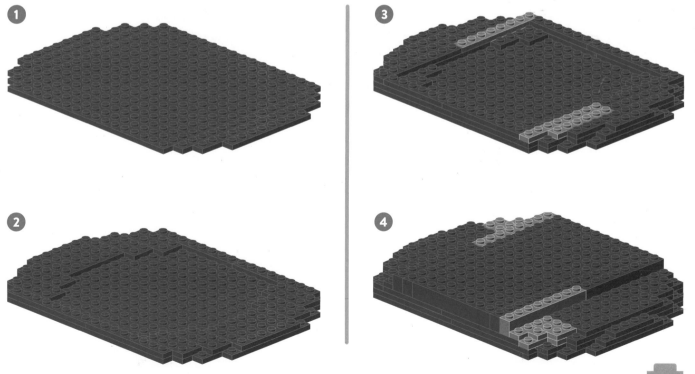

2

4

PIECES REQUIRED

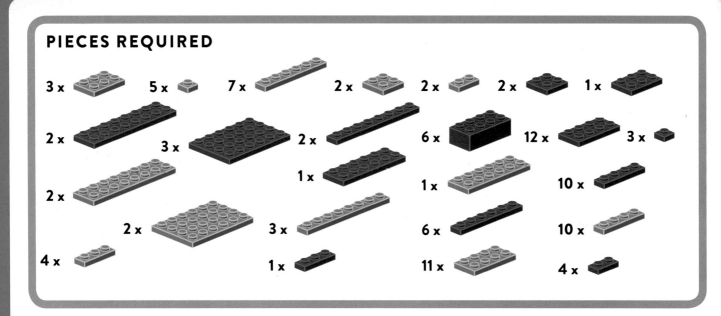

3 x   5 x   7 x   2 x   2 x   2 x   1 x

2 x   3 x   2 x   6 x   12 x   3 x

2 x   1 x   1 x   10 x

2 x   3 x   6 x   10 x

4 x   1 x   11 x   4 x

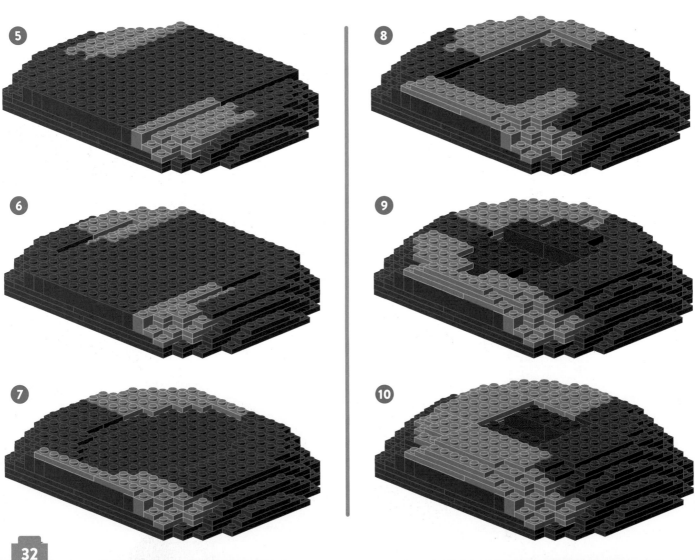

5

6

7

8

9

10

PIECES REQUIRED

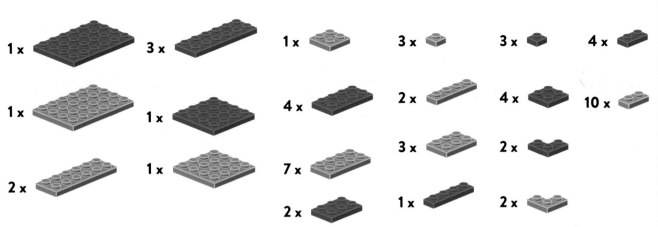

1 x
3 x
1 x
3 x
3 x
4 x

1 x
1 x
4 x
2 x
4 x
10 x

2 x
1 x
7 x
3 x
2 x

2 x
1 x
2 x

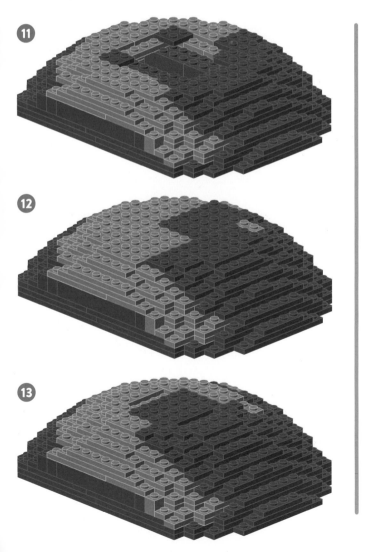

11

12

13

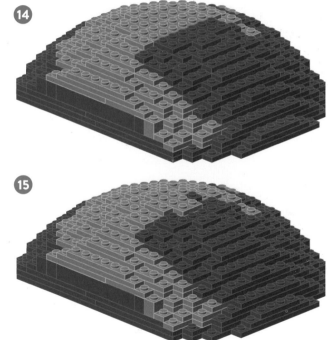

14

15

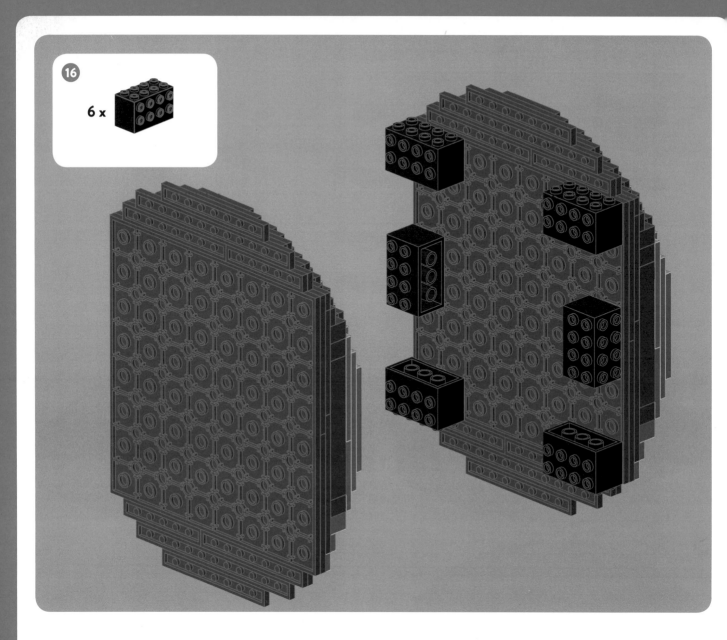

FACT

- The Earth is approximately 4.5 billion years old. It is the only known planet to support life – us!

- The Earth is the only planet in our Solar System to not have been named after a Greek or Roman God.

PART 2

PIECES REQUIRED

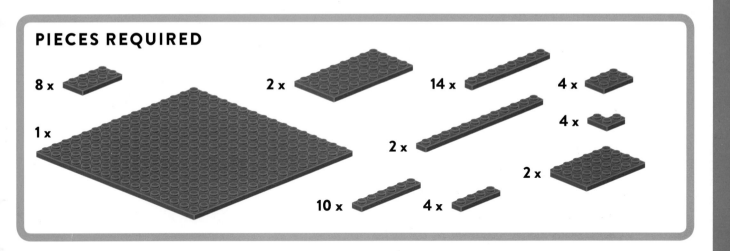

8 x

1 x

2 x

14 x

4 x

4 x

2 x

10 x

4 x

2 x

1

2

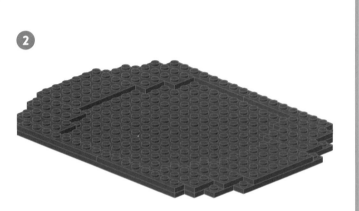

3

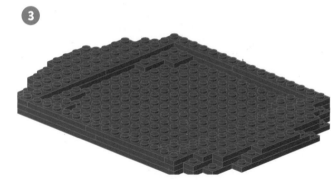

4

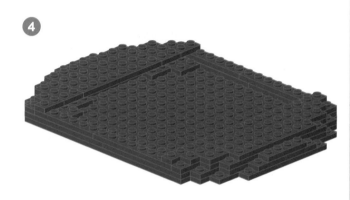

PIECES REQUIRED

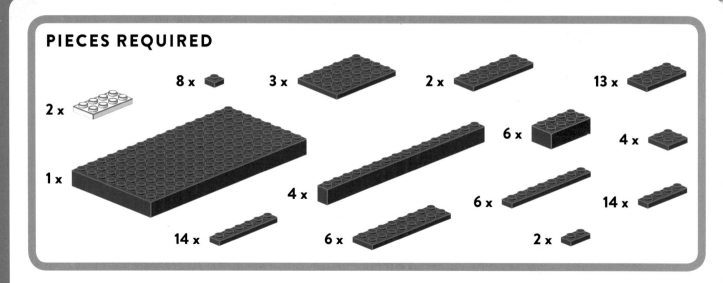

2 x

8 x   3 x   2 x   13 x

1 x   6 x   4 x

4 x   6 x   14 x

14 x   6 x   2 x

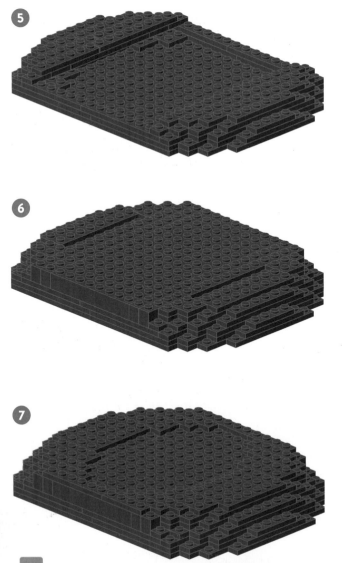

5

6

7

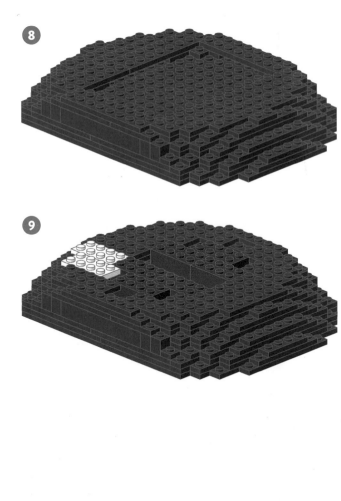

8

9

PIECES REQUIRED

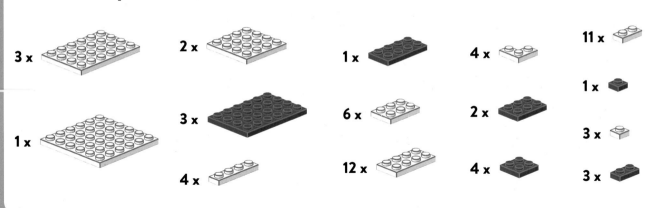

3 x

2 x

1 x

4 x

11 x

1 x

3 x

6 x

2 x

1 x

12 x

4 x

3 x

4 x

3 x

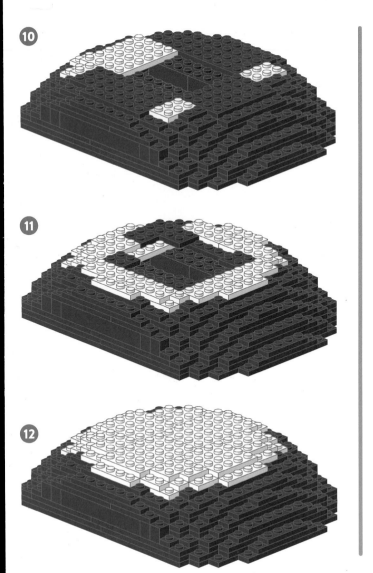

10

11

12

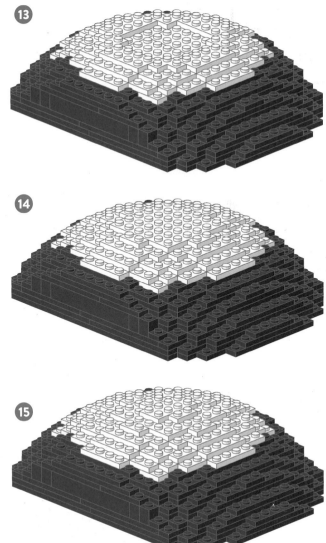

13

14

15

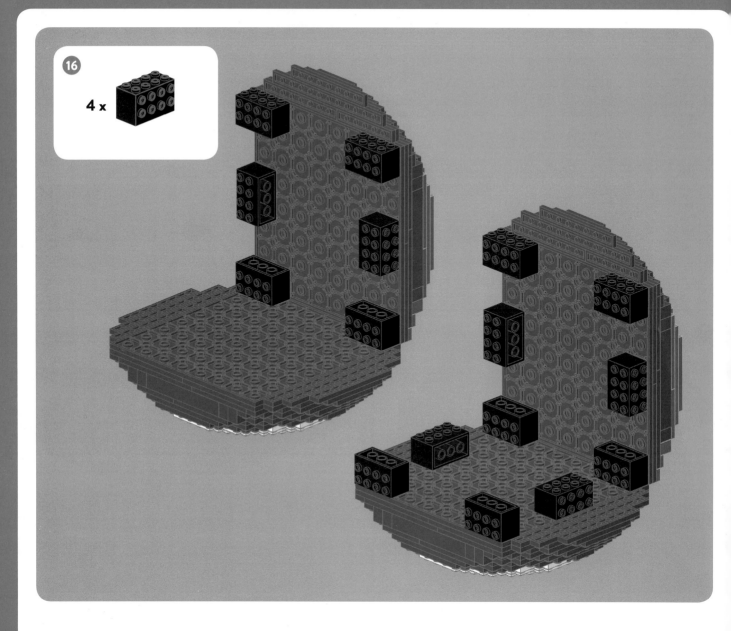

16

4 x

FACT

- Earth's equator is 40,075 kilometres (24,901 miles) long. It would take a person two full years to walk that far – and that's if you walked for twelve hours a day!

- The Earth is the third planet from the sun.

PART 3

PIECES REQUIRED

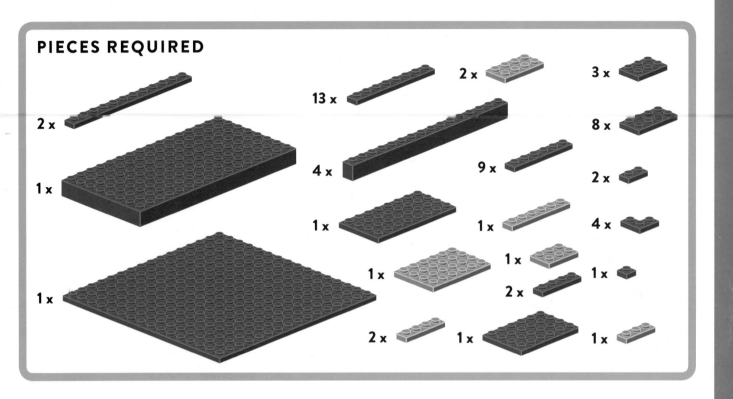

2 x
1 x
1 x
13 x
4 x
1 x
1 x
2 x
1 x
9 x
1 x
2 x
2 x
1 x
3 x
8 x
2 x
4 x
1 x
1 x
1 x

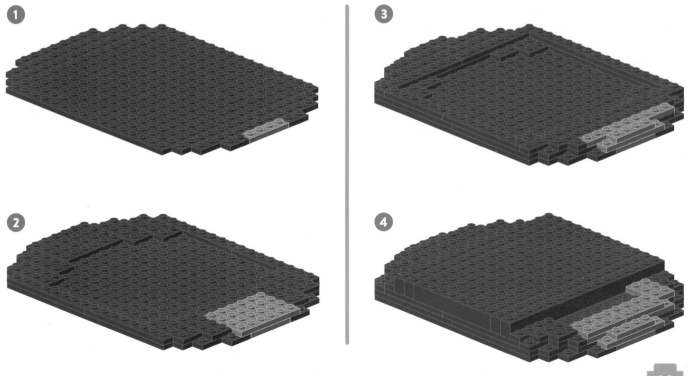

1

2

3

4

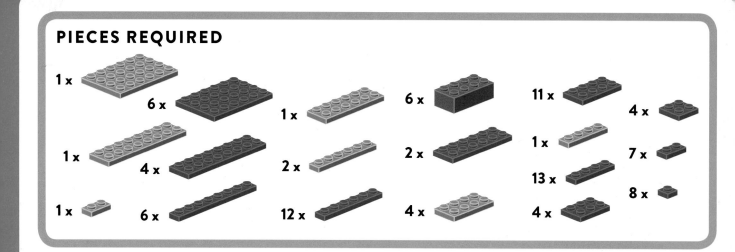

PIECES REQUIRED

1 x
6 x
1 x
6 x
11 x
4 x

1 x
4 x
2 x
2 x
1 x
7 x

1 x
6 x
12 x
4 x
13 x
4 x
8 x

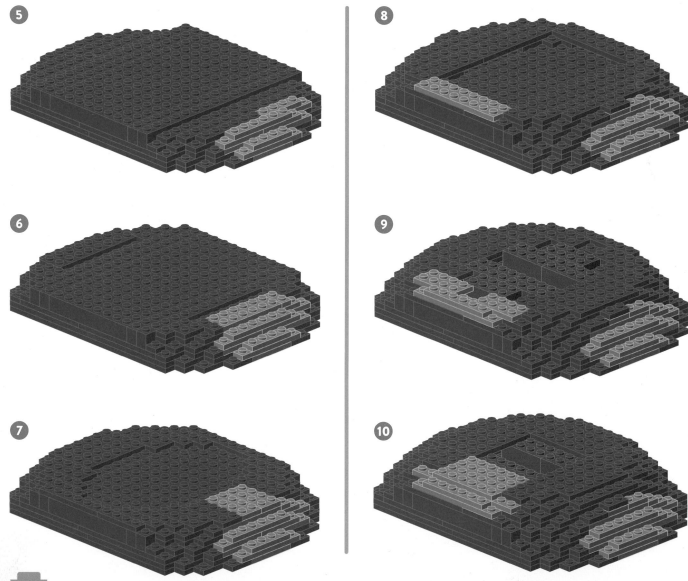

5

6

7

8

9

10

PIECES REQUIRED

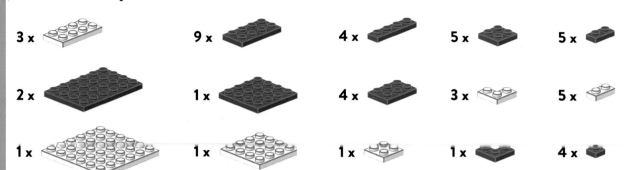

3 x   9 x   4 x   5 x   5 x

2 x   1 x   4 x   3 x   5 x

1 x   1 x   1 x   1 x   4 x

11

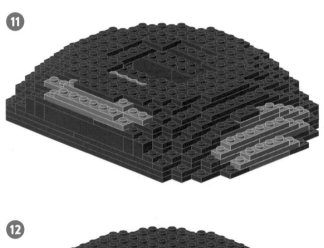

12

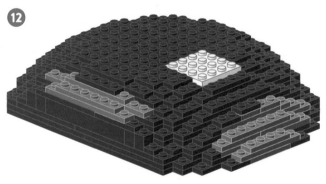

13

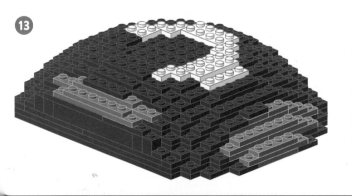

14

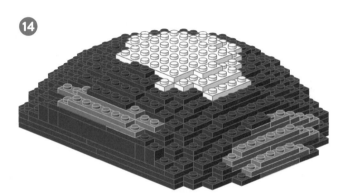

15

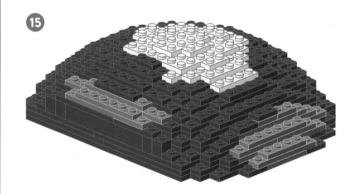

FACT

- You'll know about the moon of course, but did you know that the Earth also has two asteroids locked in its orbit? The 3753 Cruithne has a synchronized orbit with our planet (though it is actually orbiting the Sun), and the 2002AA29 makes a horseshoe orbit around the Earth.

PART 4

PIECES REQUIRED

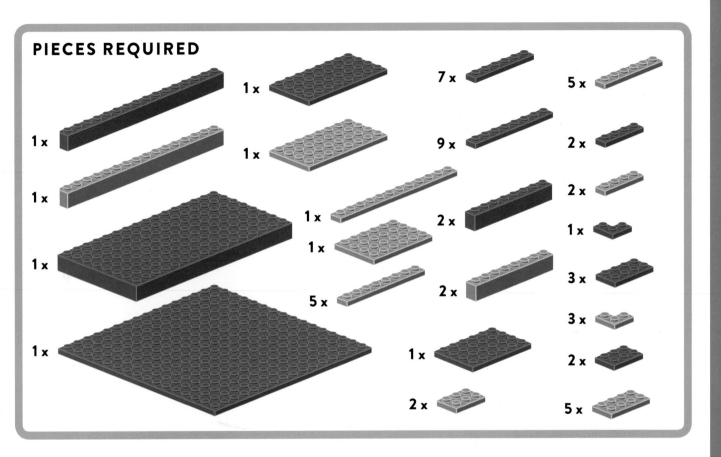

1 x
1 x
1 x
1 x

1 x
1 x

1 x
1 x
5 x

7 x
9 x
2 x
2 x
2 x

5 x
2 x
2 x
1 x
3 x
3 x
2 x
5 x

1 x

2 x

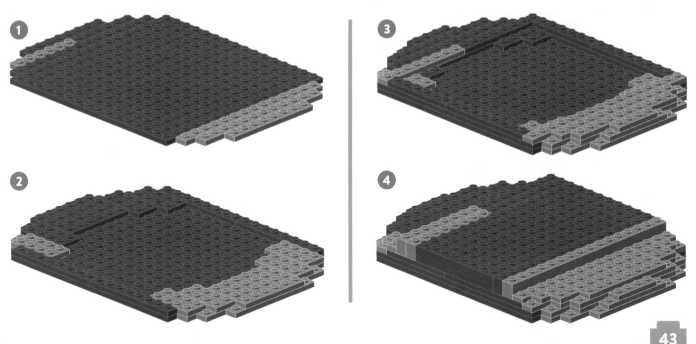

1

2

3

4

PIECES REQUIRED

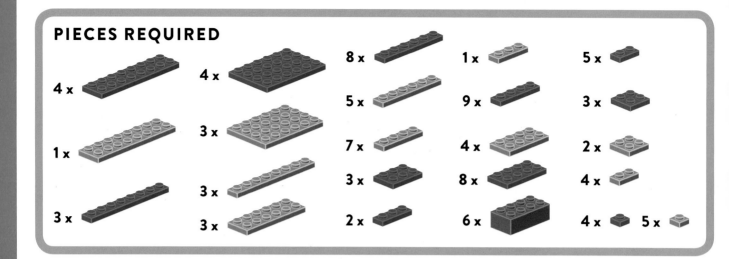

4 x   4 x   8 x   1 x   5 x

1 x   3 x   5 x   9 x   3 x

   3 x   7 x   4 x   2 x

3 x   3 x   3 x   8 x   4 x

   3 x   2 x   6 x   4 x   5 x

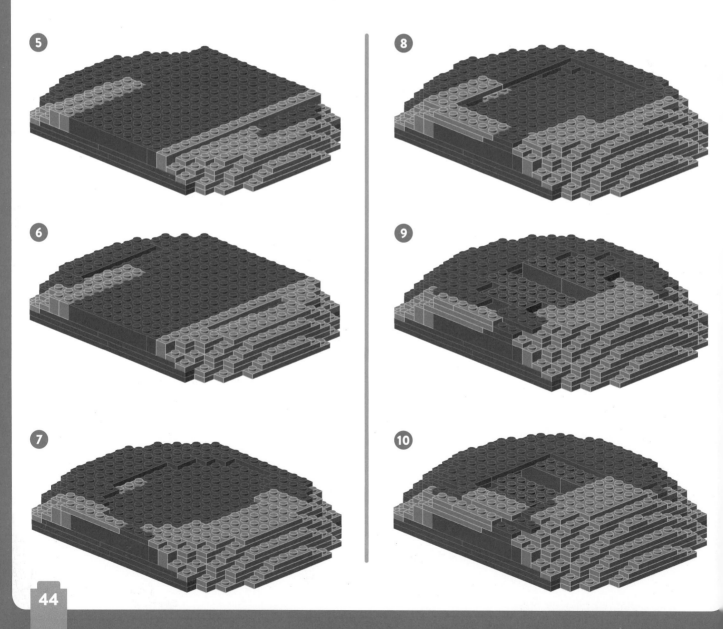

PIECES REQUIRED

3 x
1 x
10 x
1 x
3 x
2 x

2 x
11 x
4 x
6 x

1 x
1 x
4 x
3 x
3 x
3 x

1 x

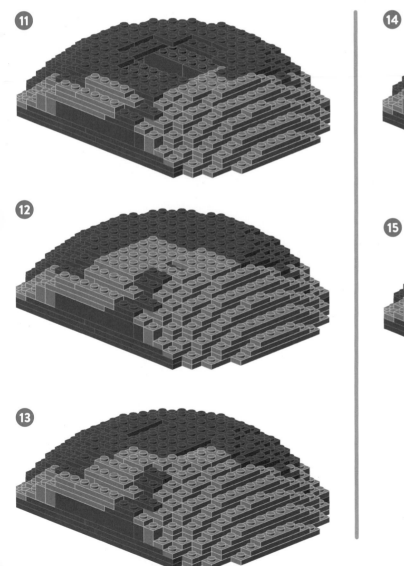

11

12

13

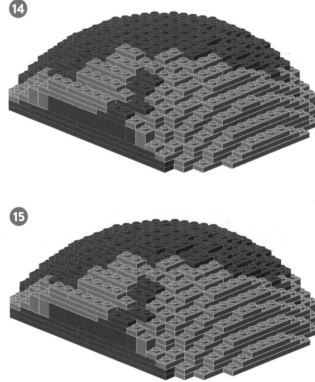

14

15

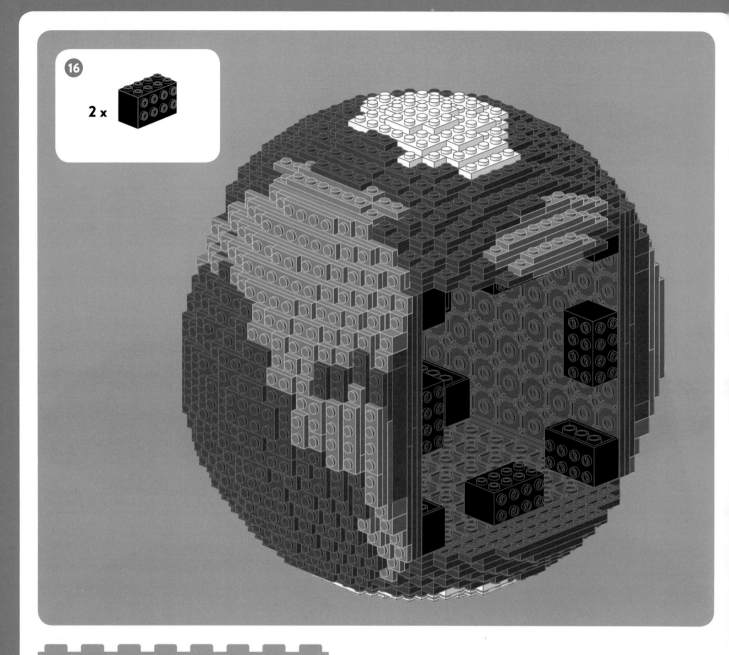

16

2 x

FACT

- Though you might feel like you're standing still, the Earth is constantly moving – the Earth spins on its axis at just over 1609 km/h (1000 mph). It also revolves around the Sun at about 107,826 km/h (67,000 mph).

PART 5

PIECES REQUIRED

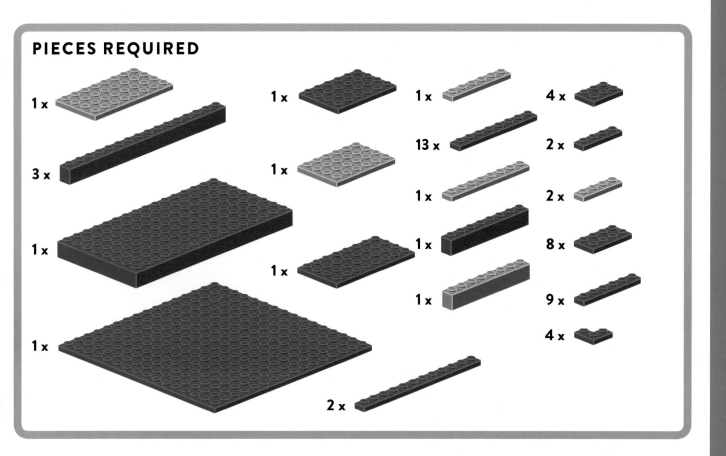

1 x

3 x

1 x

1 x

1 x

1 x

13 x

1 x

1 x

1 x

4 x

2 x

2 x

8 x

9 x

4 x

2 x

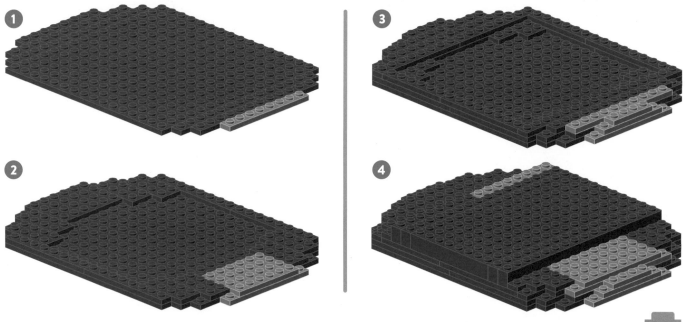

1

2

3

4

PIECES REQUIRED

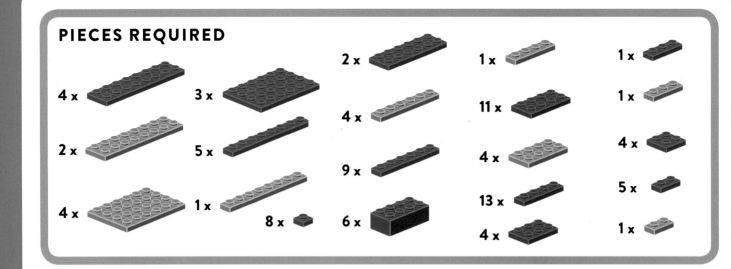

4 x

2 x

4 x

3 x

5 x

1 x

2 x

4 x

9 x

8 x

6 x

1 x

11 x

4 x

13 x

4 x

1 x

1 x

4 x

5 x

1 x

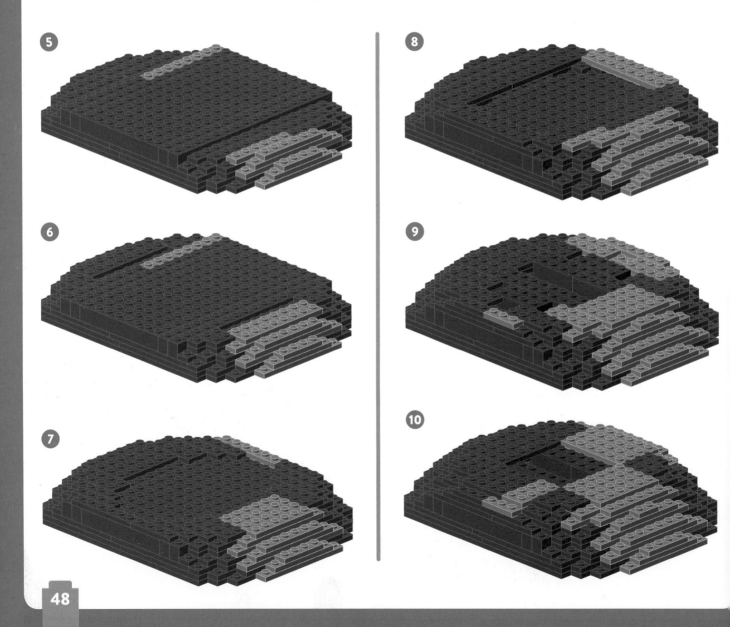

5

6

7

8

9

10

PIECES REQUIRED

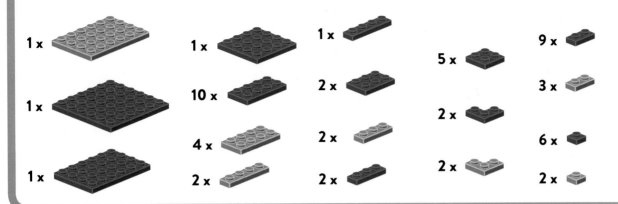

1 x
1 x
1 x

1 x
10 x
4 x
2 x

1 x
2 x
2 x

5 x
2 x
2 x

9 x
3 x
6 x
2 x

11

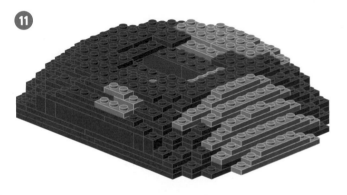

12

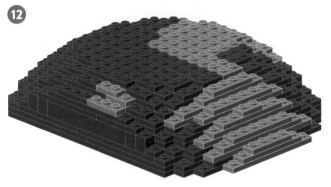

13

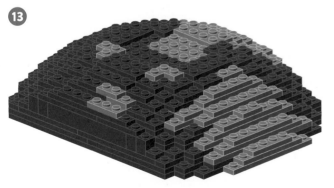

14

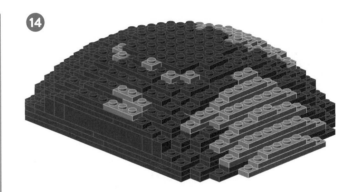

15

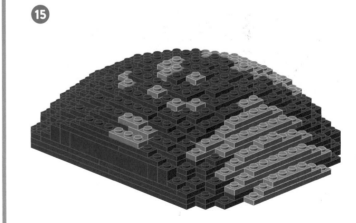

PIECES REQUIRED

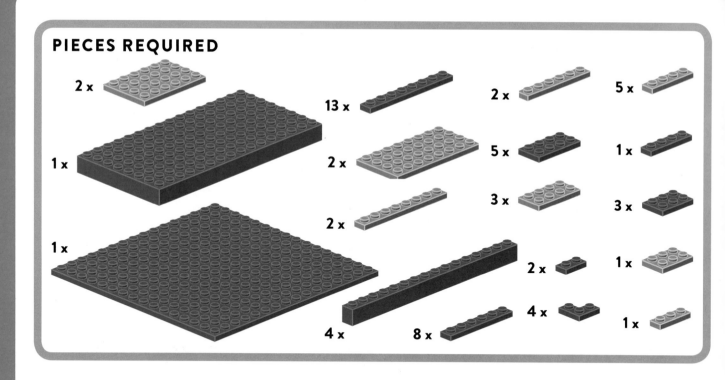

2 x

1 x

1 x

13 x

2 x

2 x

4 x

8 x

2 x

5 x

3 x

2 x

4 x

5 x

1 x

3 x

1 x

1 x

16

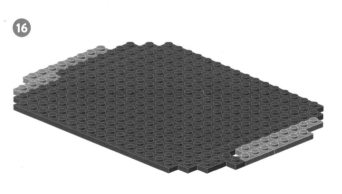

17

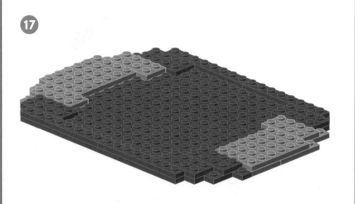

18

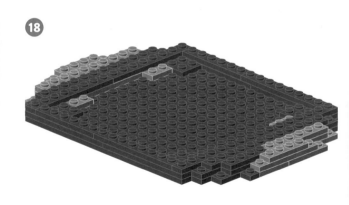

19

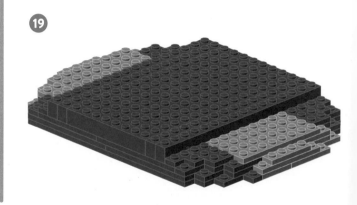

PIECES REQUIRED

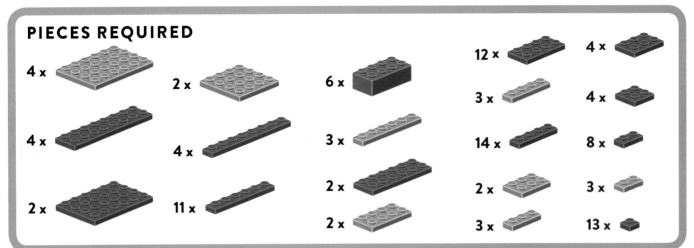

4 x

2 x

6 x

12 x

4 x

4 x

4 x

3 x

4 x

2 x

3 x

14 x

8 x

11 x

2 x

2 x

3 x

3 x

13 x

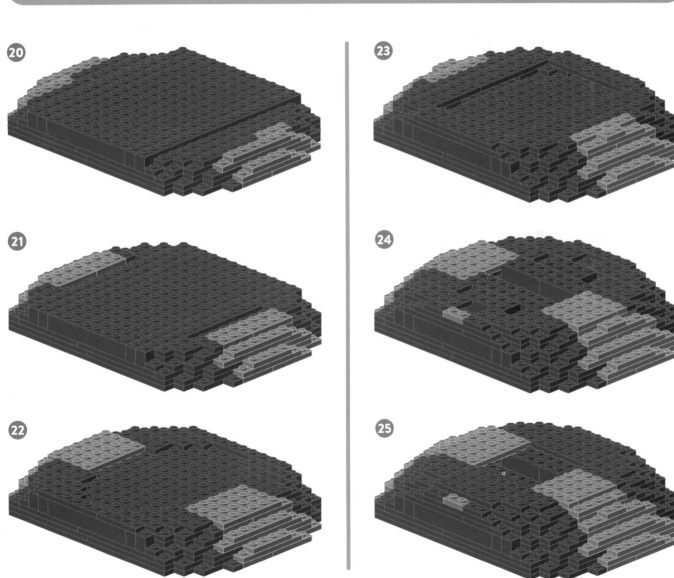

20

21

22

23

24

25

PIECES REQUIRED

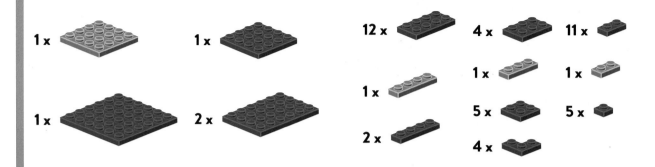

1 x   1 x

12 x   4 x   11 x

1 x   1 x   1 x

2 x   5 x   5 x

4 x

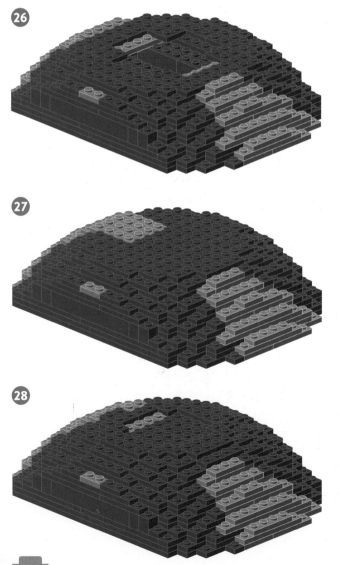

26

27

28

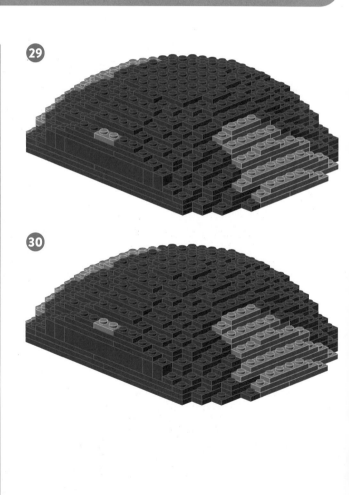

29

30

31

Carefully add the side built in part five to the build to finish the sphere.

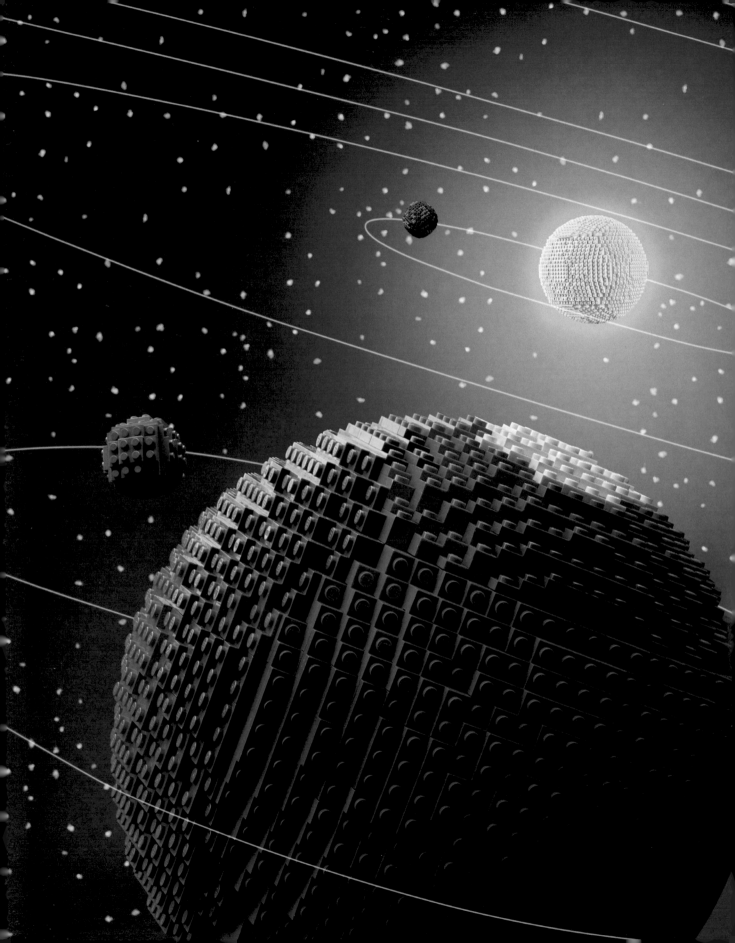

SATURN'S RINGS

PIECES REQUIRED

4 x   12 x   4 x   4 x   84 x   4 x

1

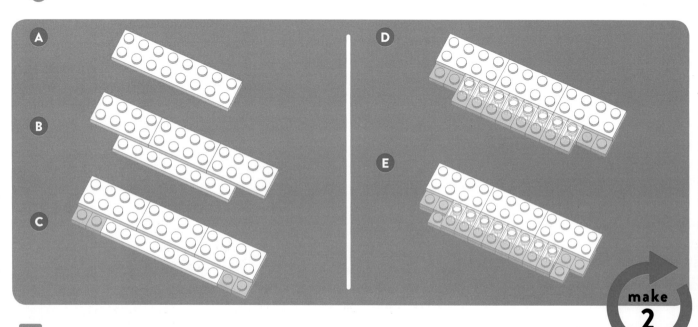

A

B

C

D

E

make
2

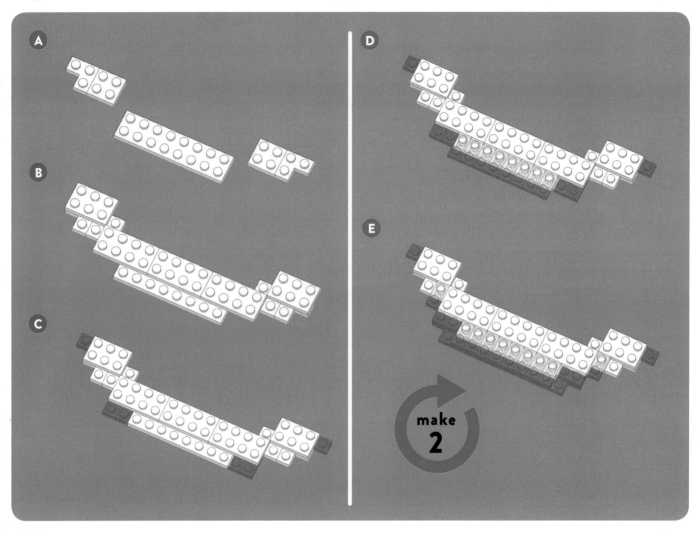

A

B

C

D

E

make
2

Attach all four pieces as pictured, then
carefully slide the finished build over the top
of Saturn and gently push to the middle.

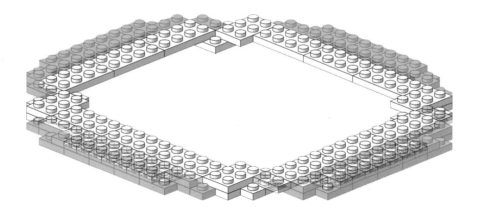

TELESCOPES

Humans have always gazed at the stars in the night sky. In 1609, the Italian astronomer Galileo Galilei (1564–1642) was the first person to turn his telescope to the stars, seeing these distant objects more clearly for the first time. Since then, telescopes have been responsible for many of our most extraordinary discoveries about the Universe.

TELESCOPES ON EARTH

Optical telescopes use curved mirrors and lenses to gather light from far away objects, making them appear closer and brighter. Today, the largest optical telescope is the Gran Telescopio Canarias on the island of La Palma, Spain. It is 10.4 metres (410 in) wide and its vision is 4 million times more powerful than the human eye's. Powerful optical telescopes are usually located in observatories in deserts or on mountaintops, where there are fewer clouds and less interference from city lights.

The Hubble Space Telescope shows an image of the star cluster NGC 1854, located around 135,000 light years away.

Radio telescopes do not collect light; they collect radio waves. Many objects in the Universe do not emit enough light to be seen through an optical telescope, but they do emit energy in the form of radio waves. Whether it is day or night, cloudy or clear, radio telescopes collect the radio waves emitted from distant objects such as pulsars, quasars, and galaxies.

An Observatory dome watches the skies from the summit of the Mauna Kea volcano, Maui, Hawaiian islands. Mauna Kea hosts the world's largest astronomical observatory, with telescopes operated by astronomers from 11 countries.

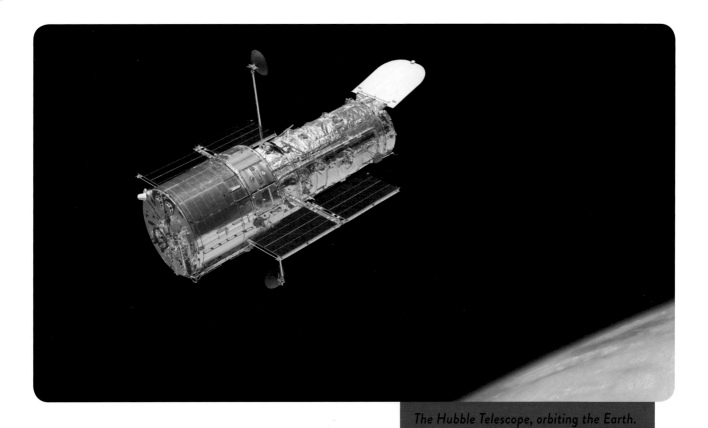

SPACE TELESCOPES

Space telescopes are not on Earth: they are in orbit around the Earth or Sun. Luckily for us, damaging waves of energy from space, such as infrared, ultraviolet, and X-rays, are blocked by the atmosphere of our planet. But this also stops ground-based telescopes from studying objects that emit those forms of energy. By sending telescopes high above our atmosphere, they get an amazingly clear view.

The first successful space telescope was NASA's OAO-2-Stargazer. Launched in 1968, it carried 11 ultraviolet telescopes. It discovered the clouds of hydrogen gas around comets. Today, NASA has three Great Observatories in orbit around Earth: Chandra, which observes X-rays; Spitzer, which observes infrared; and Hubble, which observes visible light and near-ultraviolet. Chandra has observed X-rays emitted from the black hole at the centre of our galaxy.

The James Webb Space Telescope is currently under construction. It is planned to be ready to launch in October 2018, and will orbit the Sun, 1.2 million km (7456454 miles) away from the Earth.

HUBBLE

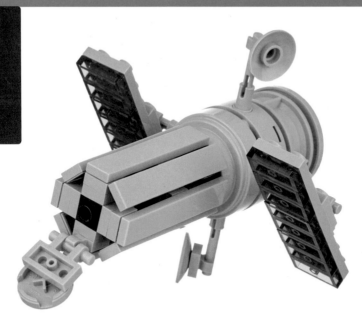

Hubble was launched in
April 1990, and has made
more than 1.2 million
observations since the
mission began.

PIECES REQUIRED

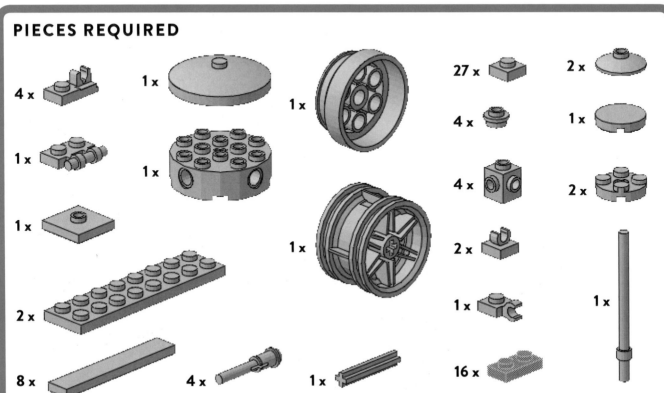

4 x

1 x

1 x

1 x

1 x

2 x

8 x

1 x

1 x

1 x

27 x

4 x

4 x

2 x

1 x

2 x

2 x

1 x

1 x

16 x

4 x

1 x

1 x

1

1 x

1 x

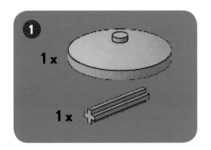

2

1 x

3

1 x

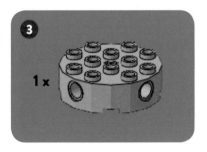

4

2 x

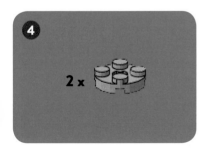

5

1 x

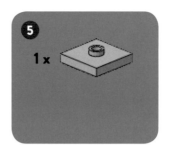

6

1 x

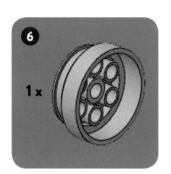

7

1 x

8

1 x

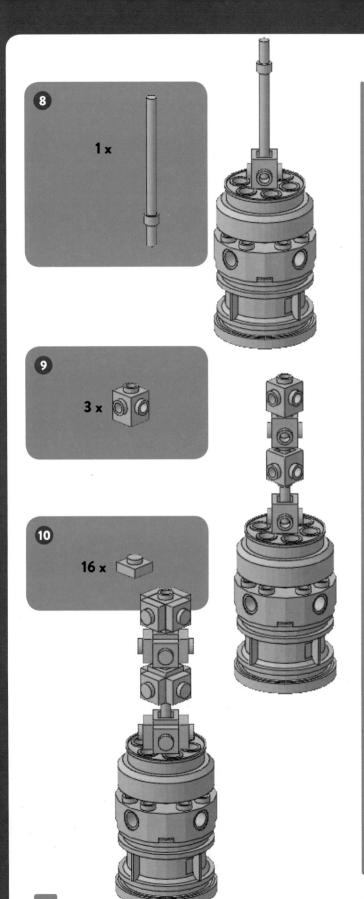

9

3 x

10

16 x

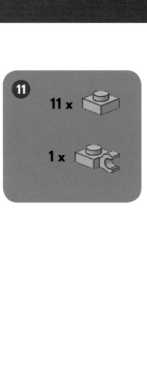

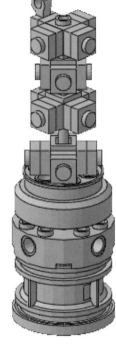

12

4 x

13

8 x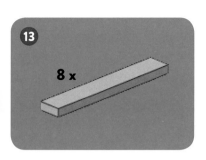

14

4 x

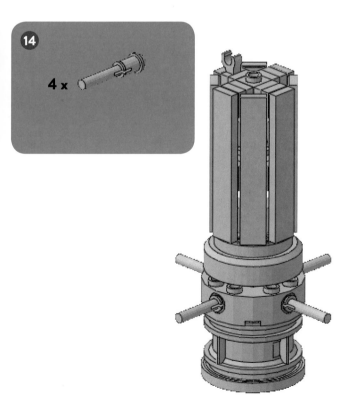

15

1 x

8 x   2 x

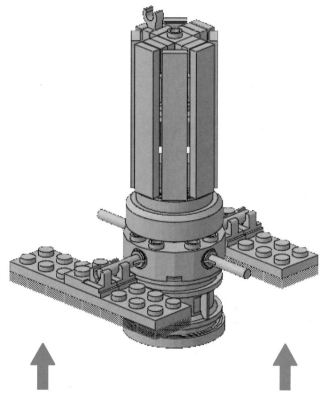

make
2

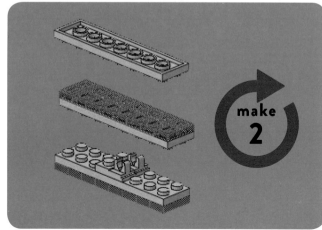

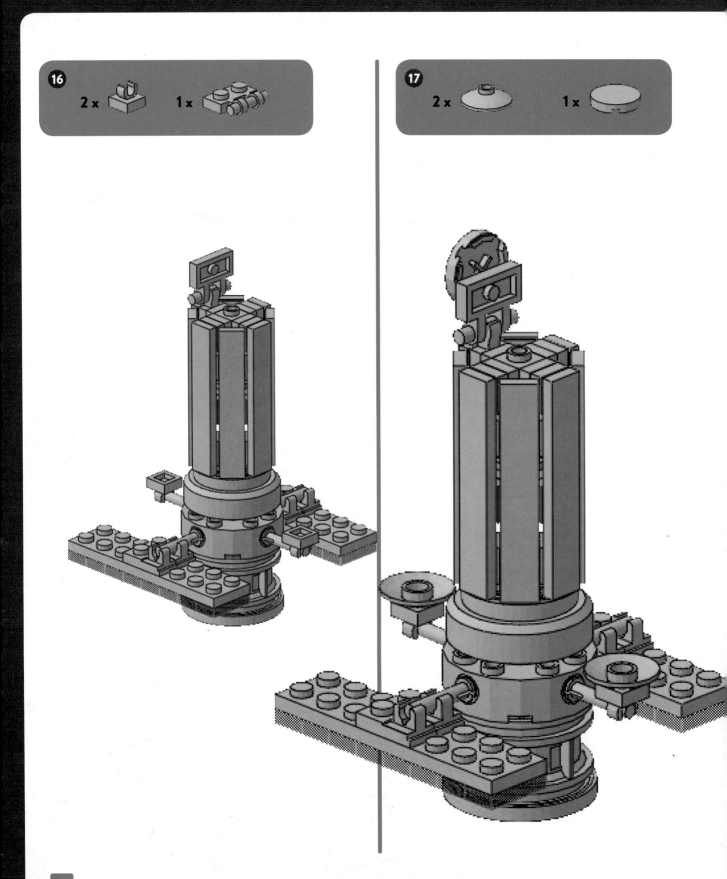

JAMES WEBB

The JWSP (James Webb Space Telescope) is a large, infared telescope and a major space obervatory.

PIECES REQUIRED

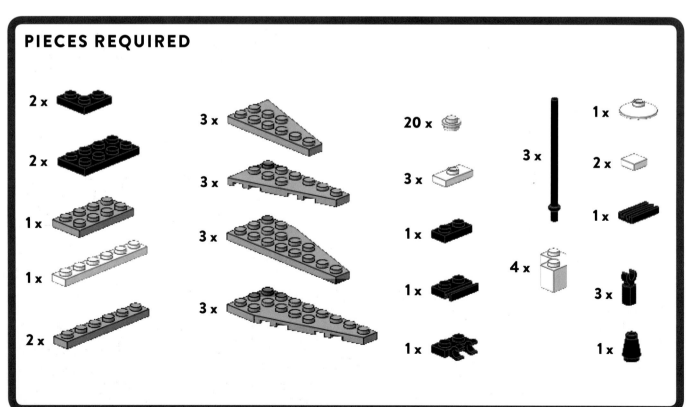

2 x
2 x
1 x
1 x
2 x

3 x
3 x
3 x
3 x

20 x
3 x
1 x
1 x
1 x

3 x
4 x

1 x
2 x
1 x
3 x
1 x

PIECES REQUIRED CONTINUED

2 x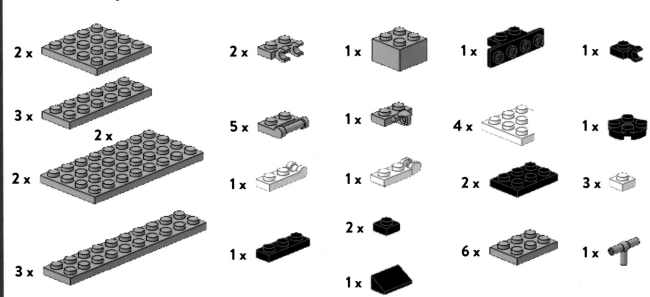
3 x
2 x
2 x
3 x

2 x
5 x
1 x
1 x

1 x
1 x
2 x
1 x

1 x

1 x
4 x
2 x
6 x

1 x
1 x
2 x
3 x
1 x

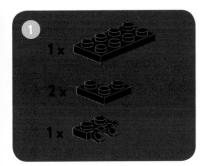
1
1 x
2 x
1 x

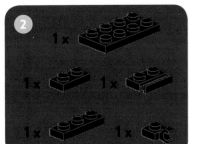
2
1 x
1 x   1 x
1 x   1 x

3
2 x

4
1 x
1 x   2 x

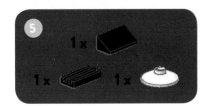
5
1 x
1 x   1 x

6

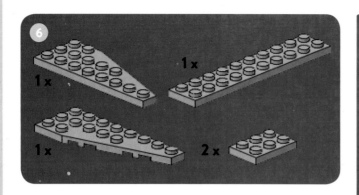

1 x

1 x

1 x

2 x

7

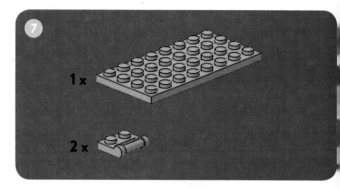

1 x

2 x

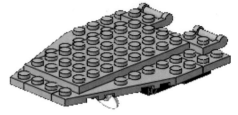

8

1 x

1 x

1 x

2 x

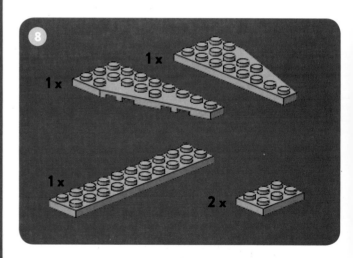

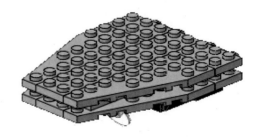

FACT

- In 1961, President John F. Kennedy put James E. Webb (1906–1992) in charge of NASA and set him the goal of sending astronauts to the Moon. Eight years later, Webb had succeeded. In honour of his work, NASA named a space telescope after him.

9

1 x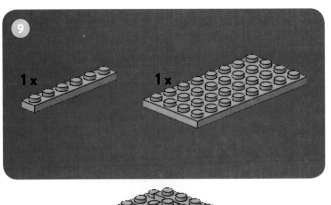

1 x

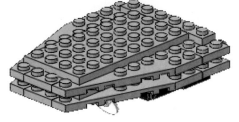

10

1 x

1 x

1 x

2 x

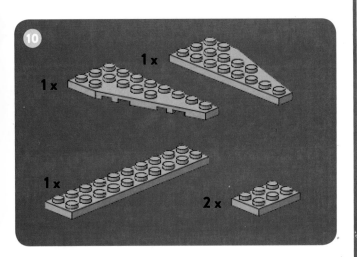

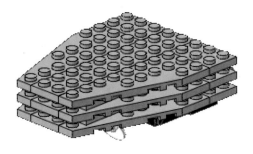

11

1 x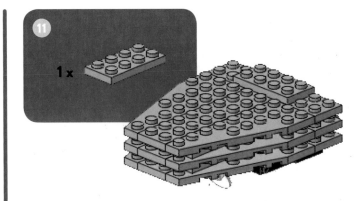

12

2 x

13

2 x

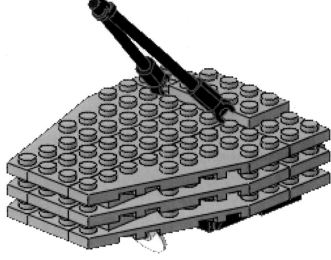

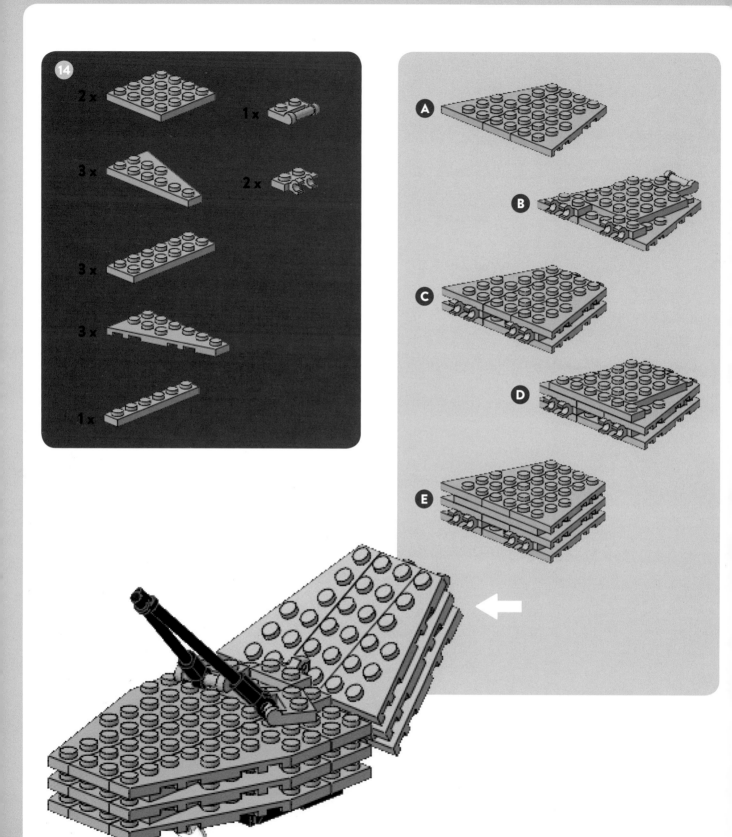

15

1 x

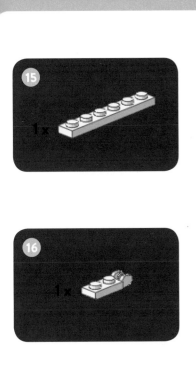

16

1 x

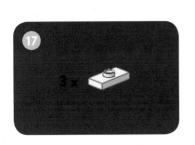
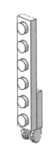

17

3 x

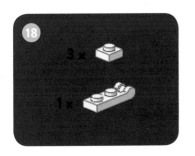

18

3 x

1 x

19

2 x

1 x

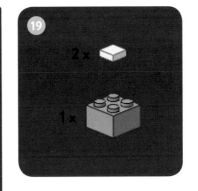
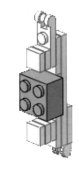

20

4 x

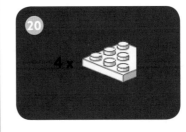
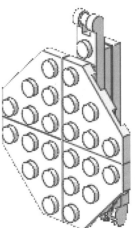

21

4 x

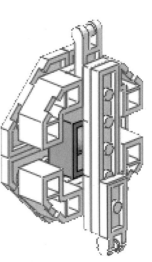

22

1 x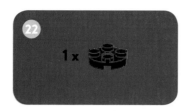

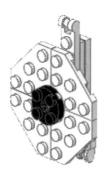

24

1 x

1 x

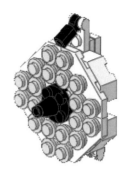

23

20 x

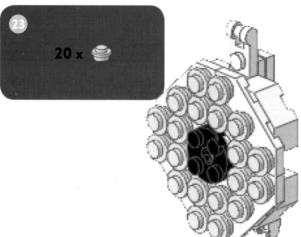

25

1 x

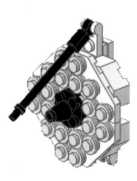

FACT

- The James Webb Space Telescope cost $9 billion to build. After it reaches its orbit around the Sun in 2018, the telescope will study the earliest galaxies and stars that formed just a few hundred million years after the Big Bang.

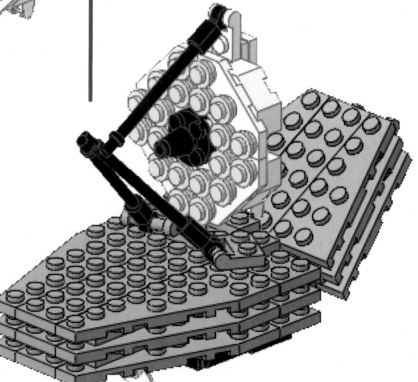

PROBES

A probe is a robotic, unmanned spacecraft that is sent into space to explore the Solar System or beyond. Space probes can study places that are too far away or too hostile for astronauts. Probes are armed with equipment that allows them to take photographs, collect samples, run scientific tests, and send back information to Earth.

PROBE FIRSTS

There are three types of probes: interplanetary probes, orbiters, and landers. Interplanetary probes fly by moons and other planets, or leave the Solar System and head into interstellar space. The earliest of these probes was NASA's Mariner 2, which flew past Venus in 1962, transmitting information about the planet's atmosphere. When Mariner 9 entered Mars's orbit in 1971, it became the first space probe to orbit another planet.

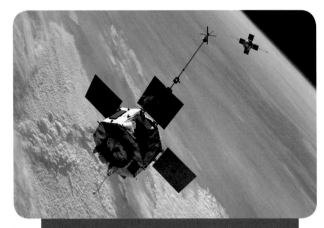

The Van Allen probes will go through and sudy the inner and outer radiation belts.

The Soviet Union's Venera 7 probe was the first to soft-land on another planet when it touched down on the surface of Venus in 1970.

The probe's descent was slowed by parachute, so it was able to transmit data back to Earth for 20 minutes. Lunokhod 1, launched by the Soviet Union, was the first successful remote-controlled rover when it travelled 10.5 km (6.5 miles) across the surface of the Moon in 1970–71.

The Cassini-Huygens is an unmanned spacecraft sent to explore the planet Saturn. It is the first probe sent to Saturn that has entered the planet's orbit – it has even landed on one of Saturn's moons!

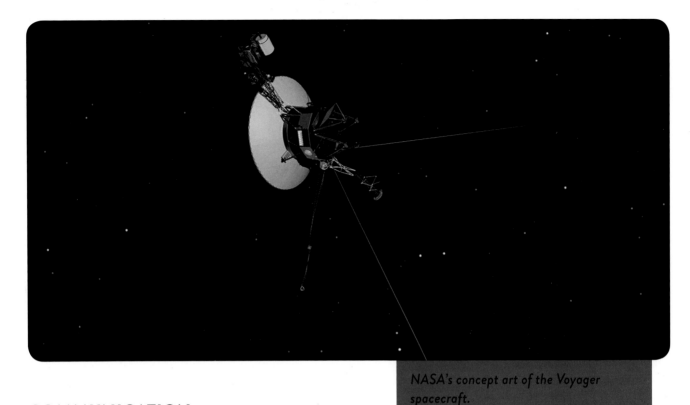

COMMUNICATION

Many probes make one-way journeys, never returning home. They transmit information back to Earth using radio waves. NASA space probes communicate with Earth using the Deep Space Network. These huge radio antennae are widely spaced on Earth, in the USA, Spain, and Australia, so that at least one can observe each space probe at all times, as our planet turns. They receive information from probes, track them, and send commands.

NASA's Apollo 11 was the first probe to return samples to Earth when it carried home 22 kg (49 lbs) of material from the Moon's surface in 1969. In 2010, Japan's Hayabusa probe returned tiny grains of rocky material that it had collected from the asteroid 25143 Itokawa five years earlier.

VIKING 1 ORBITER

The Viking 1 Orbiter launched on 20 August 1975. It orbited Mars, collecting information about the atmosphere and released a lander to the surface.

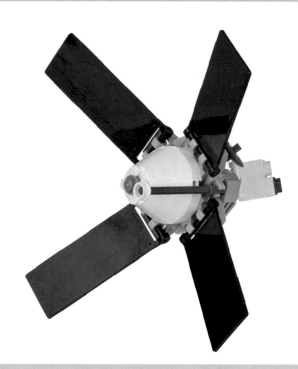

PIECES REQUIRED

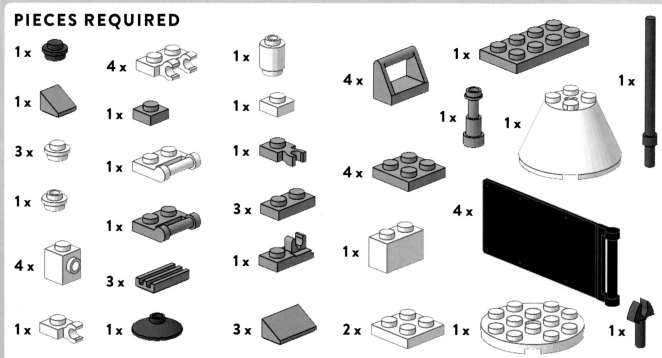

1 x
4 x
1 x
4 x
1 x
1 x

1 x
1 x
1 x
1 x
1 x

3 x
1 x
1 x
4 x

1 x
1 x
3 x
4 x

4 x
1 x
1 x
1 x

1 x
1 x
3 x
3 x
2 x
1 x
1 x

1

1 x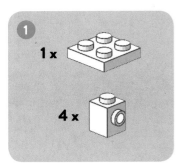

4 x

2

1 x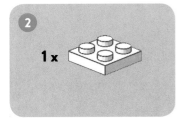

3

1 x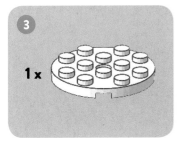

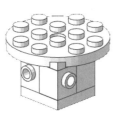

4

4 x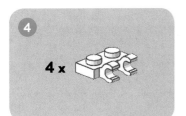

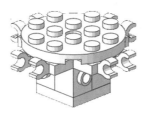

5

1 x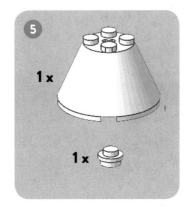

1 x

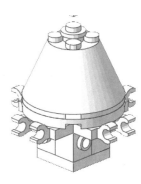

FACT

- There were two Viking orbiters: Viking 1 and Viking 2, which both went into orbit around Mars in 1975. Viking 1's gas supply ran out in 1978, but Viking 2 went on to complete 1,489 orbits before its mission ending in 1980.

6

2 x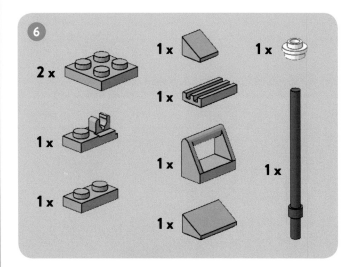
1 x
1 x
1 x
1 x
1 x
1 x
1 x
1 x

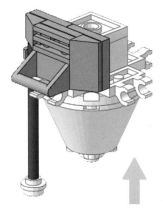

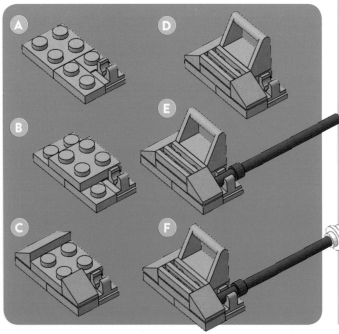

A
B
C
D
E
F

7

1 x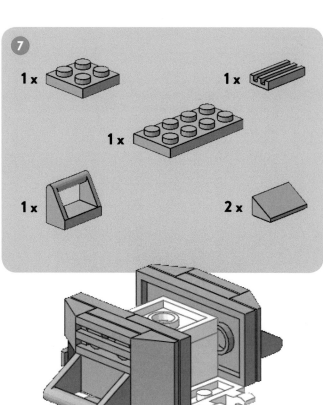
1 x
1 x
1 x
2 x

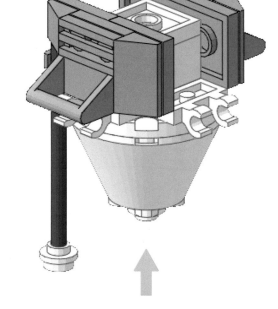

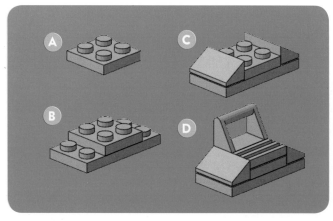

A
B
C
D

8

1 x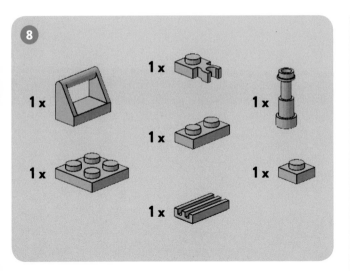

9

1 x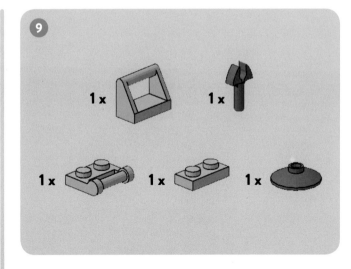

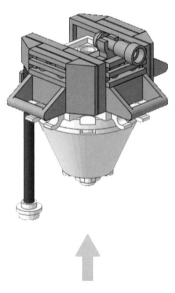

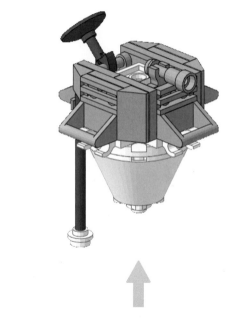

A

B

C

D

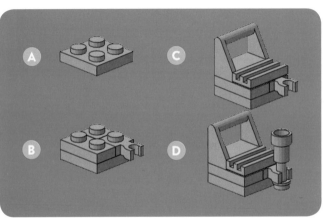

A

B

C

D

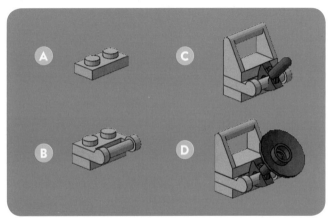

10

1 x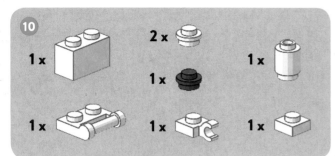
2 x
1 x
1 x
1 x
1 x
1 x

11

4 x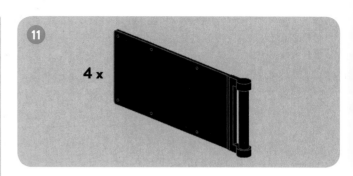

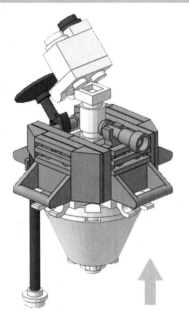

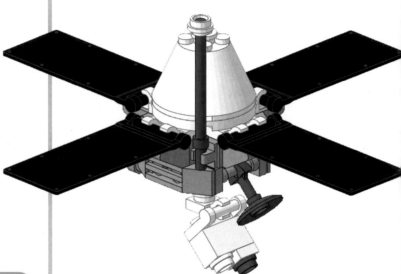

A
B
C
D
E

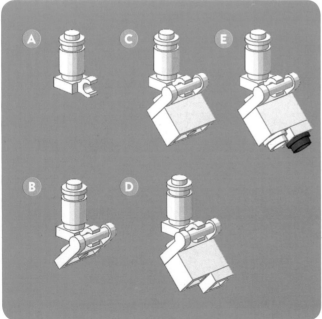

FACT

- Both Viking orbiters released a lander into Mars's atmosphere. At an altitude of 6 km (3.7 miles) and travelling at 900 km/h (600 mph), each lander opened a parachute, which slowed it enough to land on the planet without smashing to pieces.

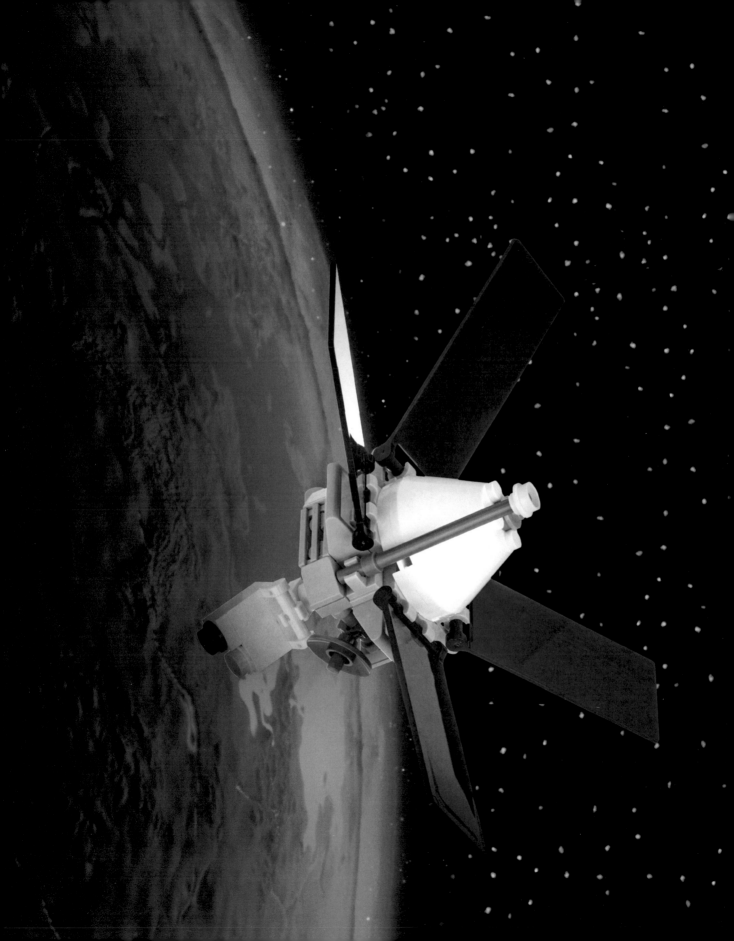

VOYAGER II

Voyager II was a space probe launched in August 1977 to study the outer planets.

PIECES REQUIRED

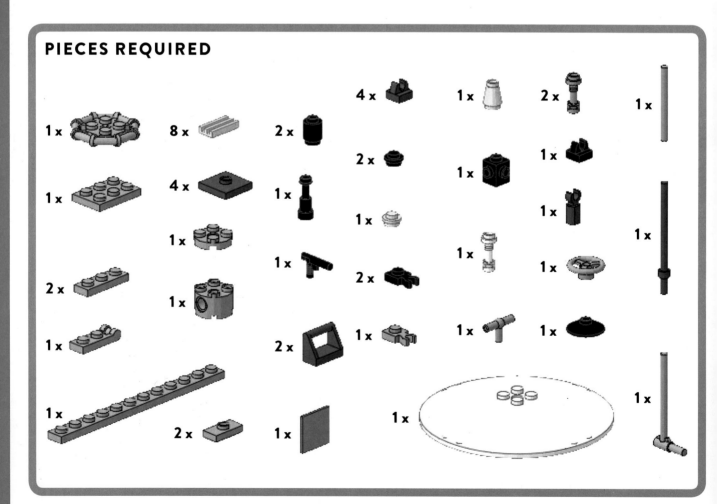

1 x
8 x
2 x
4 x
1 x
2 x
1 x

1 x
4 x
1 x
2 x
1 x
1 x

2 x
1 x
1 x
1 x
1 x
1 x

1 x
1 x
2 x
1 x
1 x
1 x

1 x
2 x
1 x
1 x
1 x

1

1 x

1 x

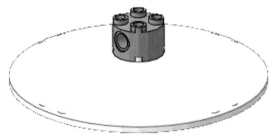

2

1 x

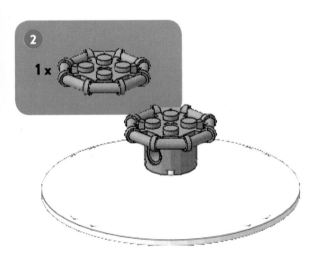

3

4 x

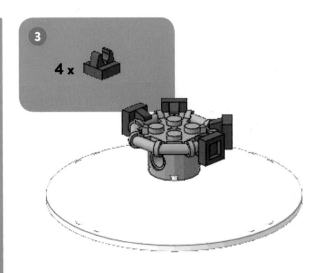

4

1 x

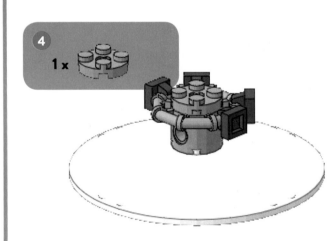

5

4 x

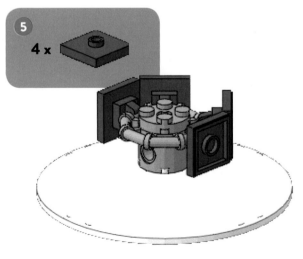

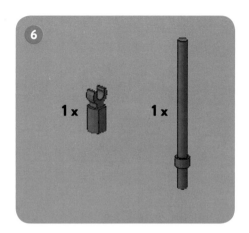

6

1 x   1 x

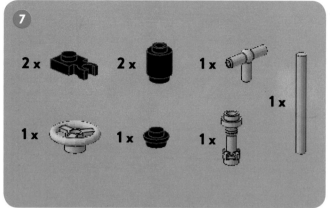

7

2 x   2 x   1 x

1 x   1 x   1 x   1 x

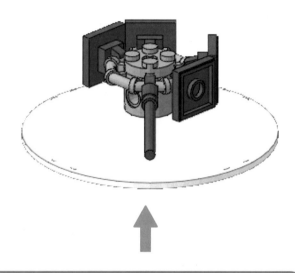

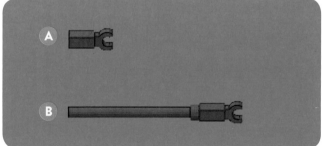

A

B

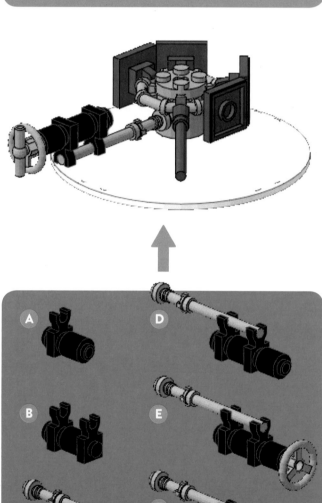

A   D

B   E

C   F

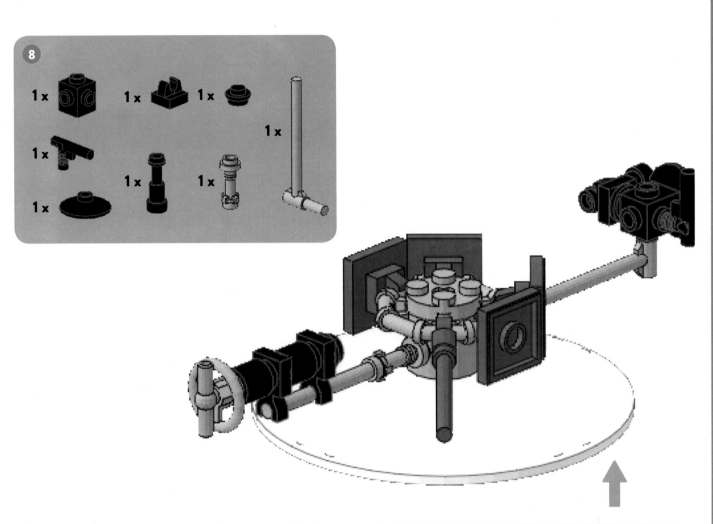

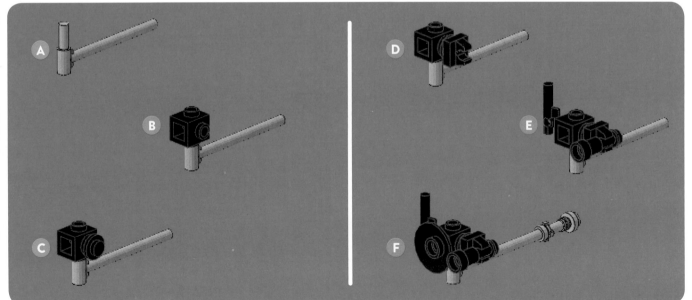

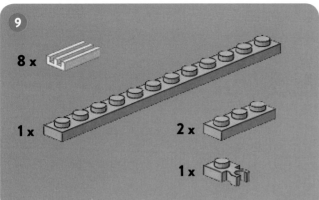

8 x

1 x   2 x

1 x

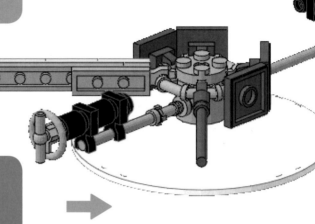

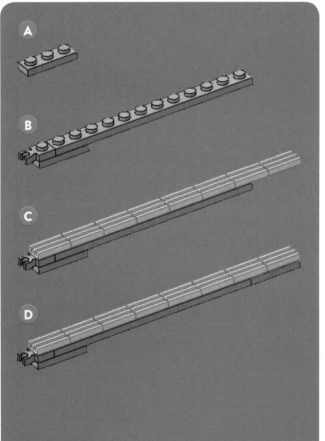

A

B

C

D

FACT

- Since leaving our Solar System, Voyager II is not making its way straight to any particular star, but in 40,000 years it should pass within 1.7 light years of the small star Ross 248.

- If all goes well, Voyager II will continue sending weak radio messages back to Earth until 2025, 48 years after its launch in 1977.

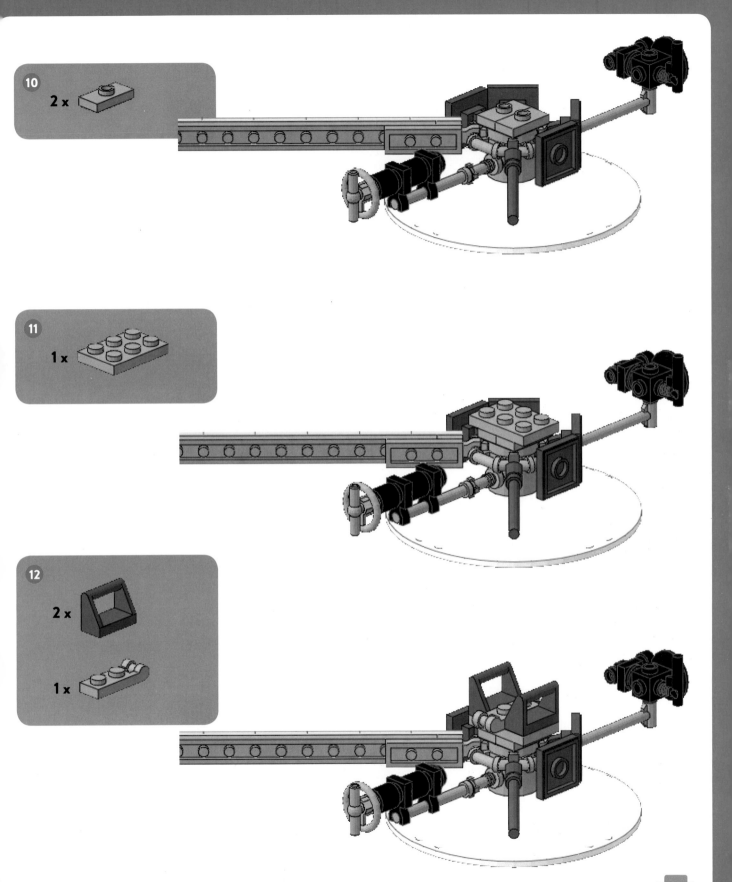

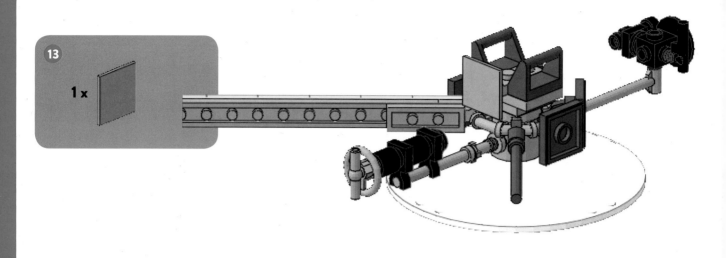

13

1 x

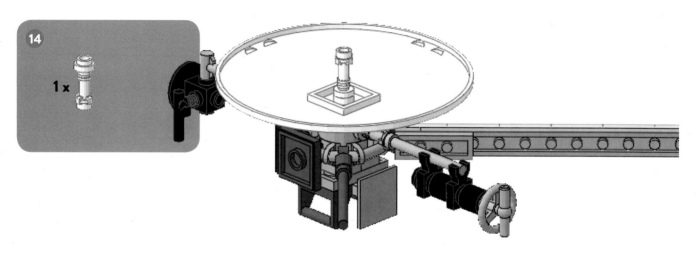

14

1 x

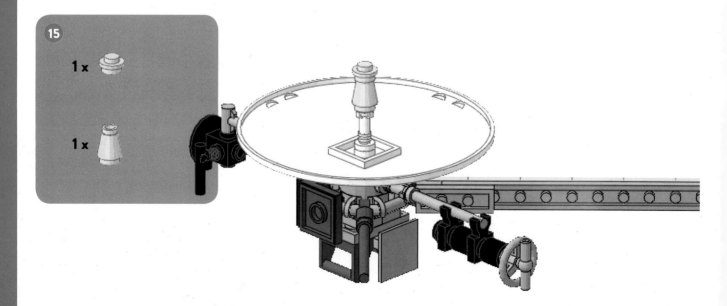

15

1 x

1 x

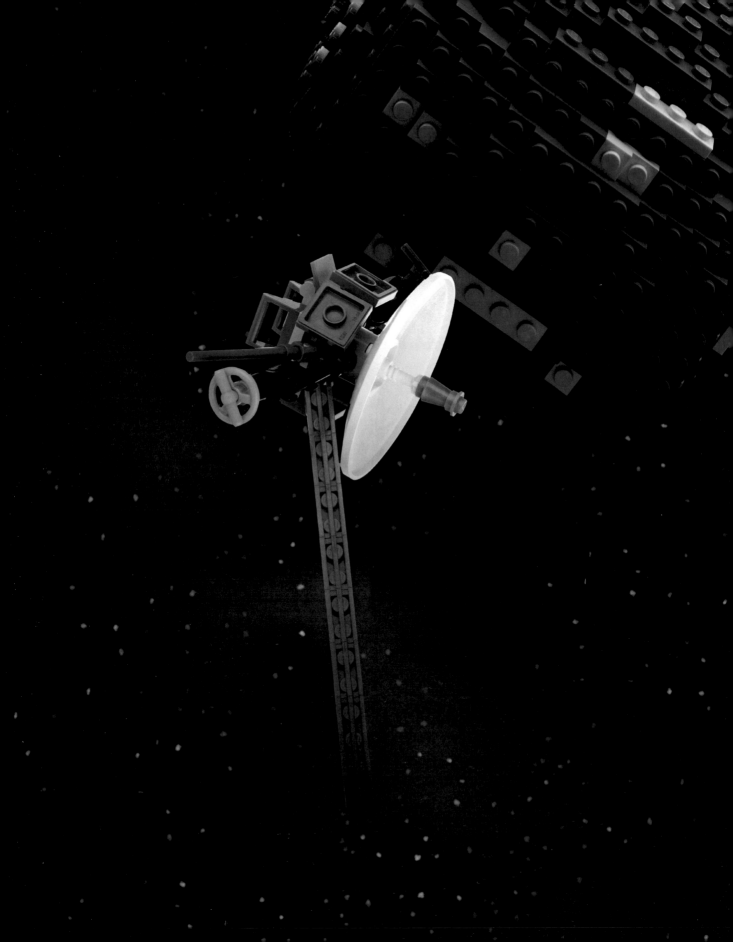

CASSINI

The Cassini-Huygens Spacecraft is an unmanned probe that has been orbiting Saturn since 2004.

PIECES REQUIRED

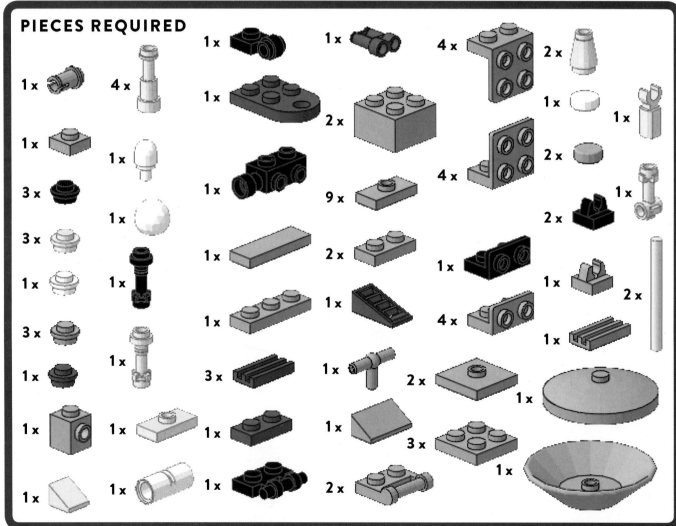

1 x   4 x

1 x   1 x   1 x   4 x   2 x

1 x   1 x   1 x

3 x   1 x   2 x   1 x

3 x   1 x   9 x   4 x   2 x

1 x   1 x   1 x   1 x

3 x   1 x   2 x   1 x

1 x   1 x   4 x   2 x

1 x   1 x

1 x   3 x   1 x   2 x   1 x

1 x   1 x   1 x   1 x   3 x

1 x   1 x   1 x   2 x   1 x

1

2 x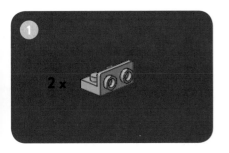

2

2 x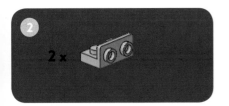

3

2 x

4

1 x

5

4 x

1 x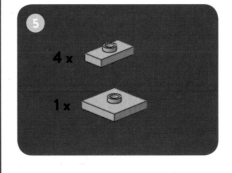

6

4 x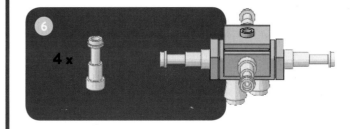

FACT

• Cassini was the first space probe to go into orbit around Saturn, in 2004. It has performed flybys of all Saturn's largest moons: Titan, Rhea, Iapetus, Dione, Tethys, and Enceladus, as well as many of its 55 smaller moons.

A

1 x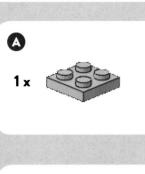

B

2 x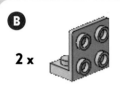

C

1 x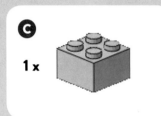

D

2 x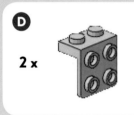

E

1 x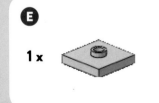

F

1 x
2 x
1 x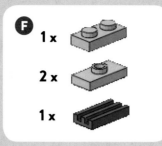
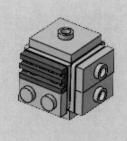

G

1 x
1 x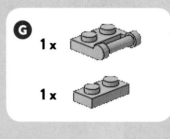

H

1 x
1 x
1 x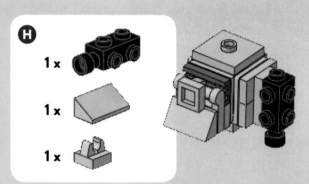

I

1 x
1 x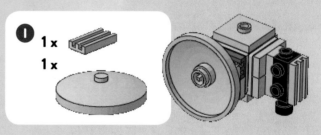

J

1 x
1 x
1 x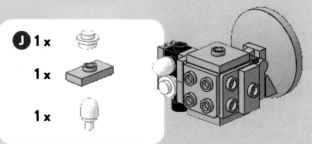

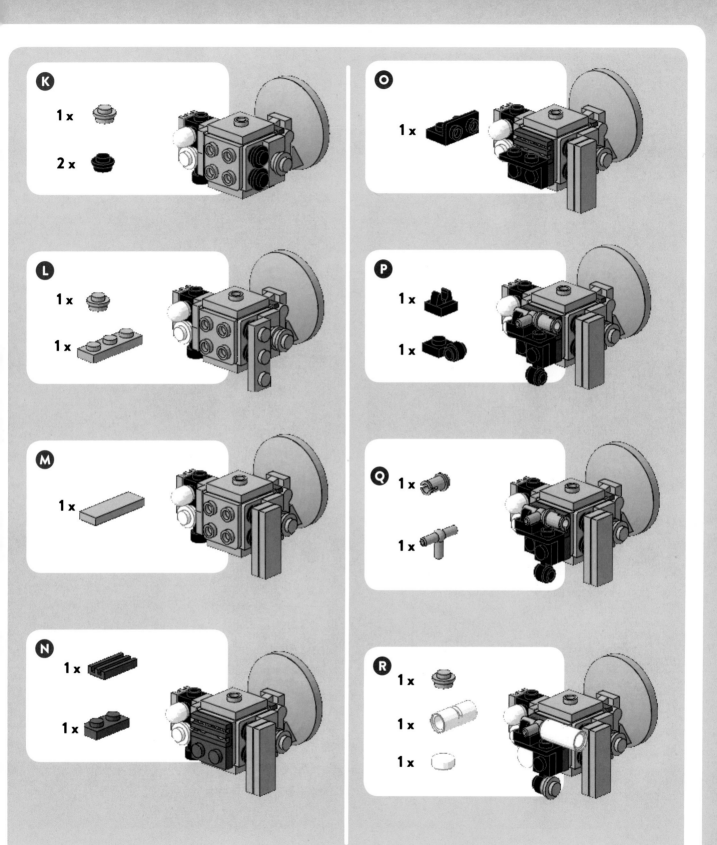

K
1 x
2 x

L
1 x
1 x

M
1 x

N
1 x
1 x

O
1 x

P
1 x
1 x

Q
1 x
1 x

R
1 x
1 x
1 x

7

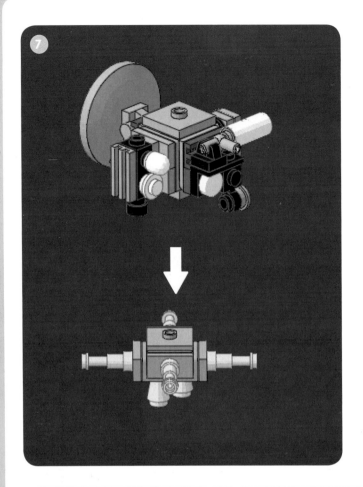

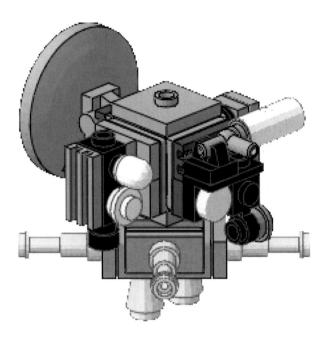

A 1 x

B 2 x

C 1 x

D 2 x

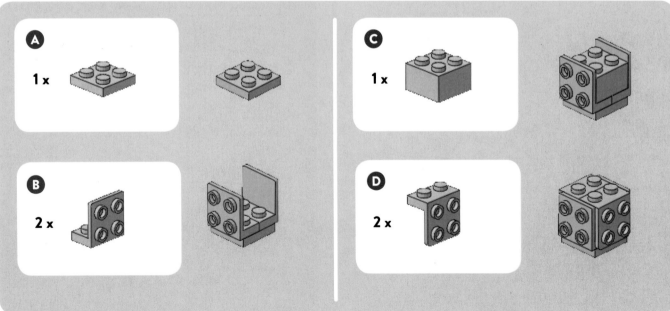

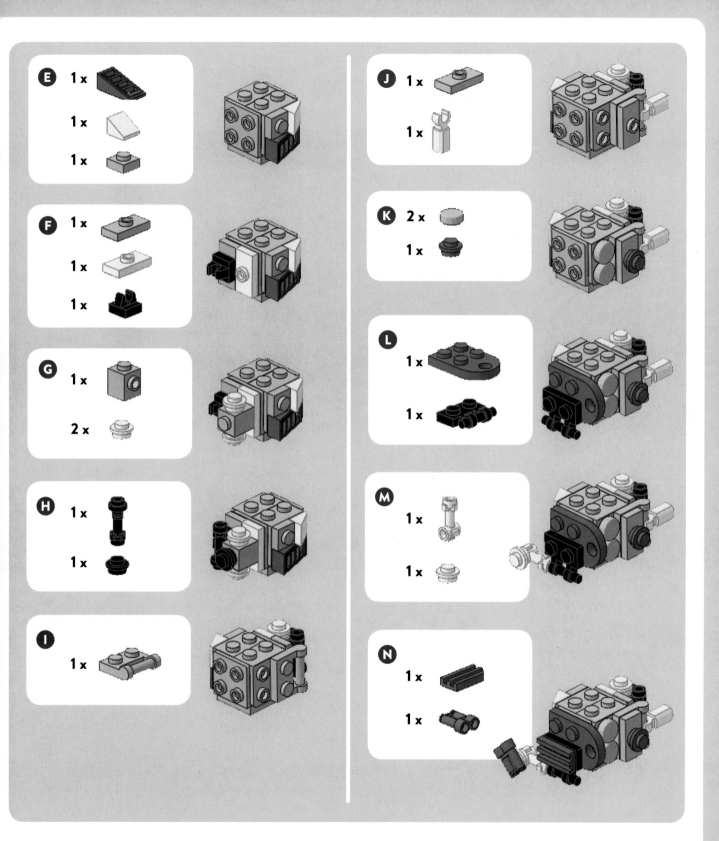

E
1 x
1 x
1 x

F
1 x
1 x
1 x

G
1 x
2 x

H
1 x
1 x

I
1 x

J
1 x
1 x

K
2 x
1 x

L
1 x
1 x

M
1 x
1 x

N
1 x
1 x

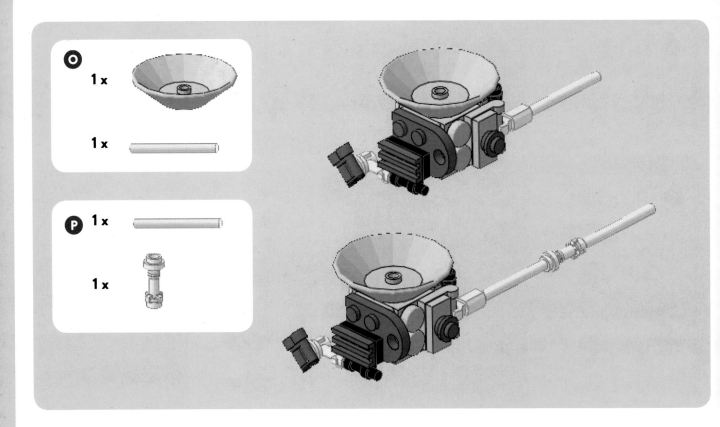

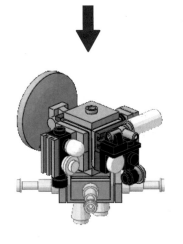

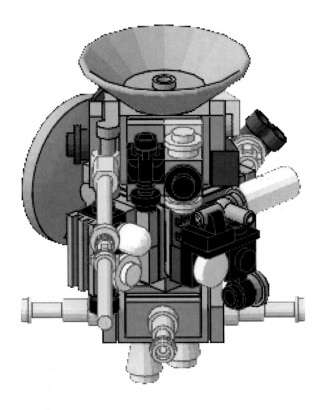

 Be very careful as you attach the last piece of this build!

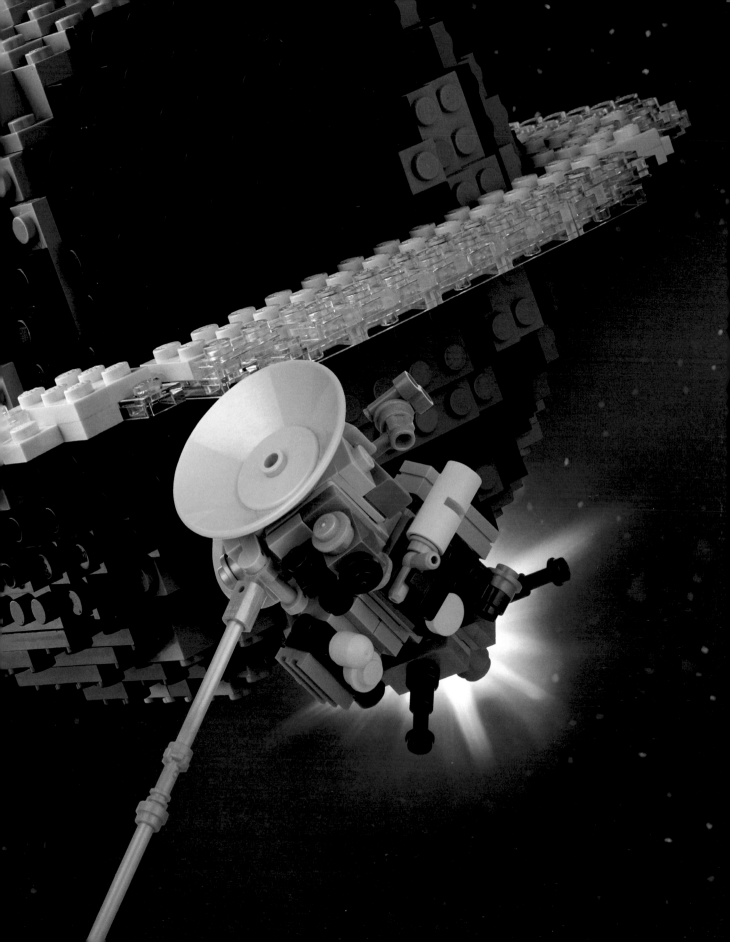

ROSETTA

The Rosetta space probe was built by the European Space Agency and launched in March 2004.

PIECES REQUIRED

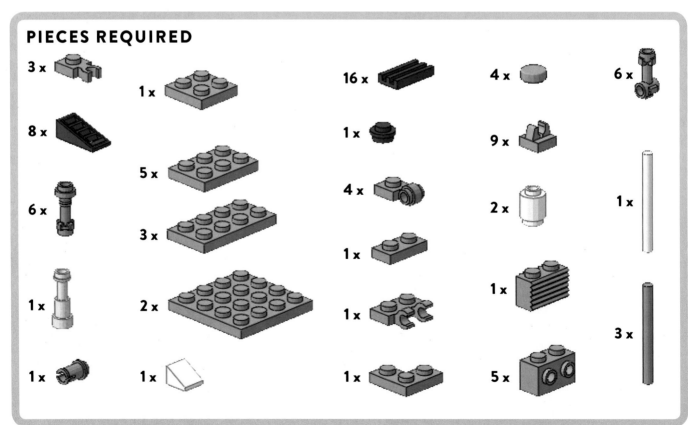

3 x

1 x

8 x

16 x

4 x

6 x

5 x

1 x

9 x

6 x

3 x

4 x

2 x

1 x

1 x

1 x

1 x

1 x

1 x

1 x

5 x

3 x

1

1 x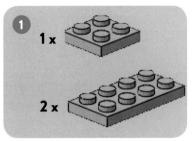

2 x

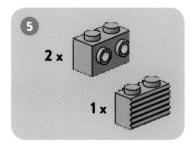

5

2 x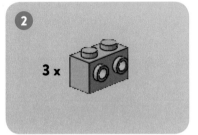

1 x

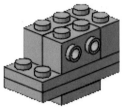

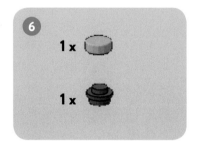

2

3 x

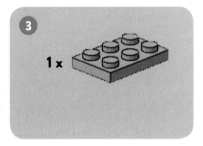

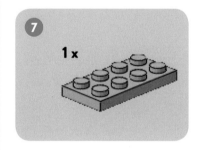

6

1 x

1 x

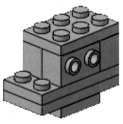

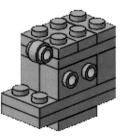

3

1 x

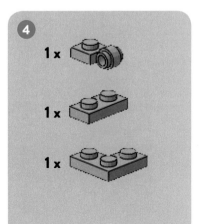

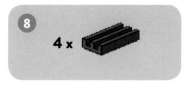

7

1 x

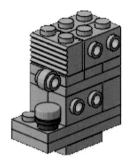

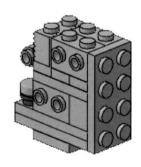

4

1 x

1 x

1 x

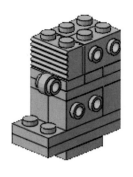

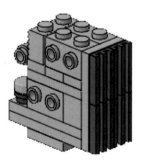

8

4 x

9

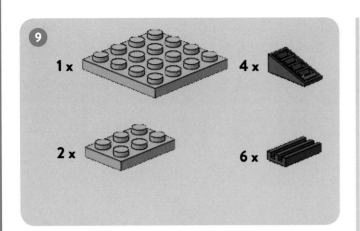

1 x
4 x
2 x
6 x

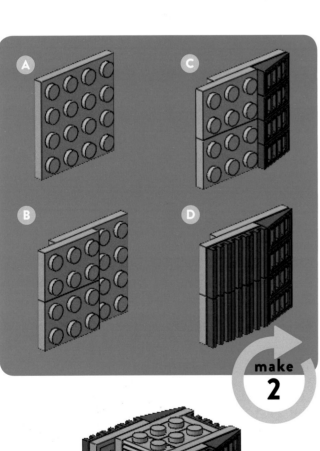

A
B
C
D

make
2

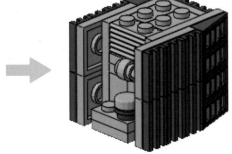

10

1 x
1 x

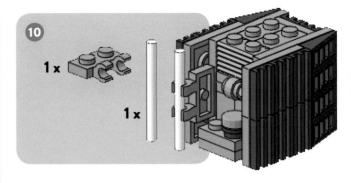

11

1 x

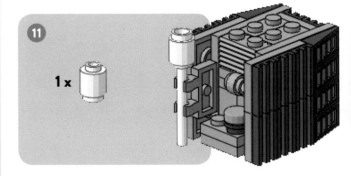

12

1 x
1 x

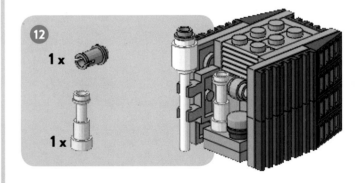

13

1 x
1 x

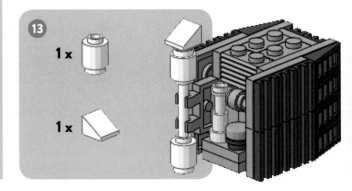

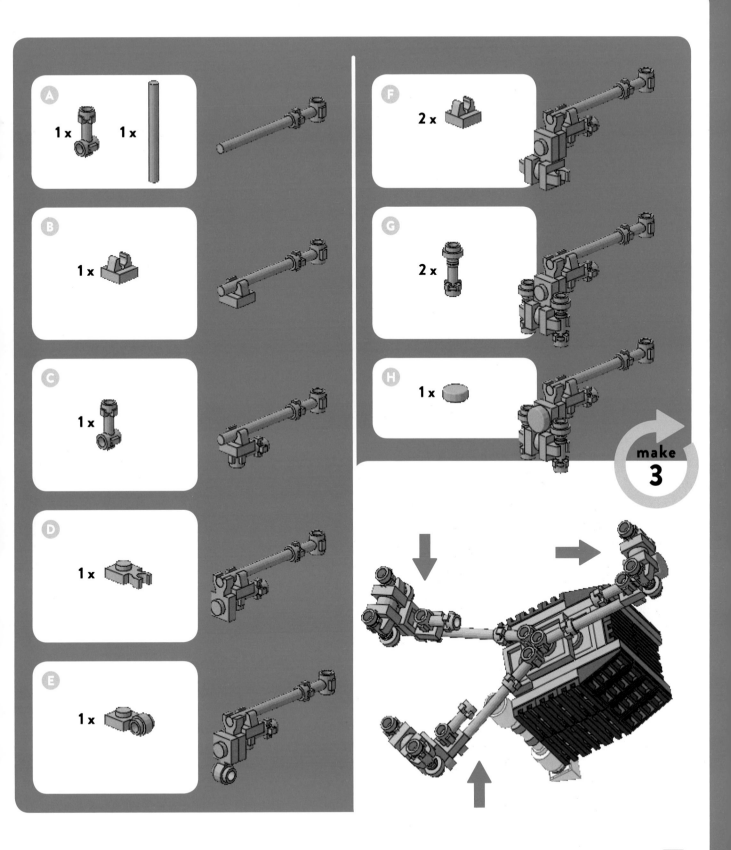

A
1 x   1 x

B
1 x

C
1 x

D
1 x

E
1 x

F
2 x

G
2 x

H
1 x

make
3

MARS CURIOSITY ROVER

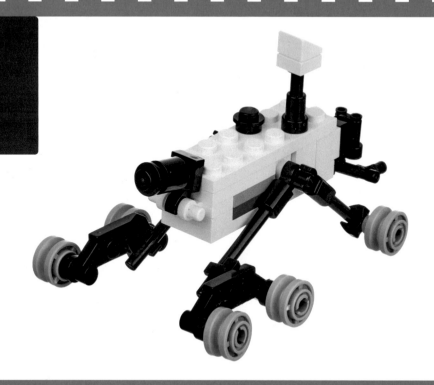

The Mars Curiosity Rover launched in 2011 and landed on Mars in 2012. It is a robotic rover sent to investigate the Martian climate and geology.

PIECES REQUIRED

1 x

1 x

1 x

1 x

5 x

1 x

4 x

1 x

1 x

2 x

4 x

2 x

1 x

2 x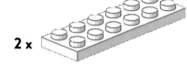

1 x

1 x

6 x

6 x

1 x

2 x

8 x

3 x

2 x

1 x

1

1 x

4 x 1 x

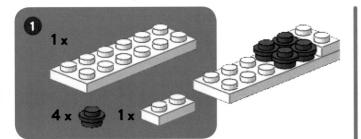

2

4 x

1 x

3

2 x

4

1 x

1 x 1 x

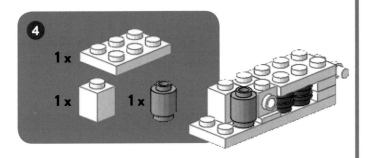

5

2 x 1 x

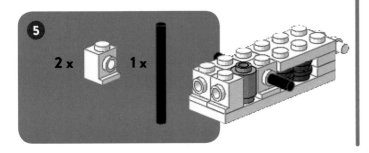

6

1 x

1 x

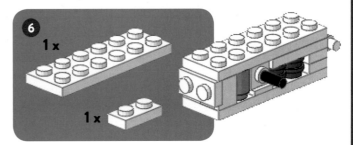

7

1 x 1 x

1 x

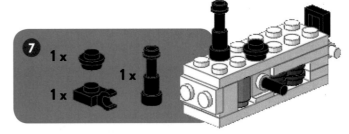

8

1 x 1 x

1 x

1 x

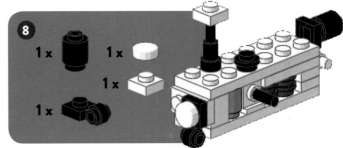

9

1 x

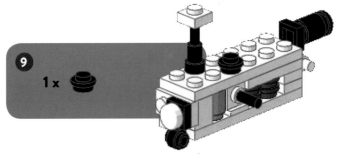

10

1 x

11

1 x

1 x

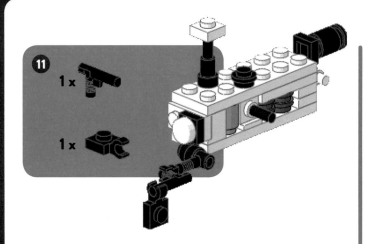

12

1 x

1 x

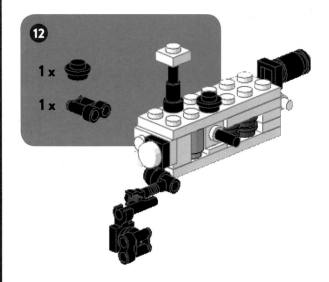

13

2 x

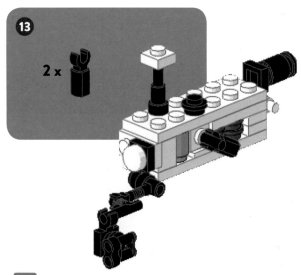

14

2 x

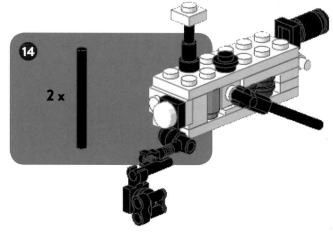

15

2 x   2 x

2 x   2 x   2 x

make

A

B

C

D

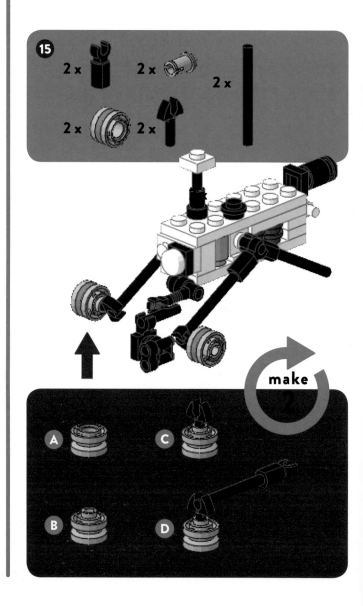

16

2 x 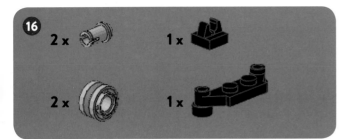 1 x

2 x 1 x

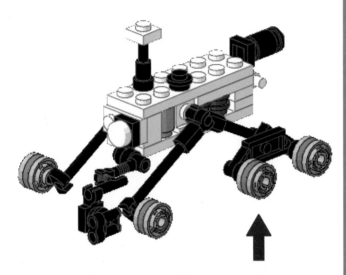

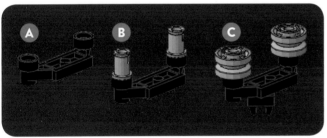

17

2 x 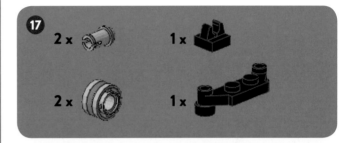 1 x

2 x 1 x

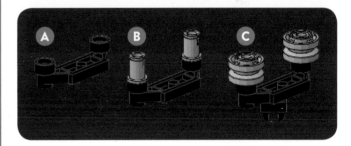

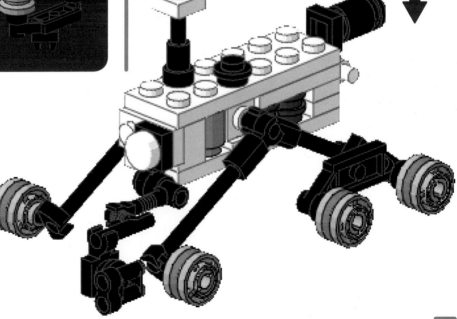

MISSION TO THE MOON

In the 1950s, the United States and Soviet Union embarked on the Space Race. These two rival countries competed to have the greatest achievements in spaceflight. The ultimate goal was to land astronauts on the Moon.

RACING FOR THE GOAL

Between 1959 and 1976, the Soviet Union launched 24 Moon probes called Luna. In 1959, Luna 2 was the first man-made object to hit the Moon. The same year, Luna 3 was the first to send home blurred photos of the far side of the Moon, giving humans their first glimpse of its cratered surface. In 1966, Luna 9 was the first probe to make a soft-landing on the Moon.

The United States was not to be left behind. From 1964, the Ranger probes sent home photos of the Moon's surface before crashing into it. In 1966 and 1967, the Lunar Orbiters mapped the Moon's surface, looking for possible landing sites. With the Apollo program, the United States began to inch ahead.

In 1968, Apollo 8 was the first manned craft to leave Earth orbit when it ferried three astronauts around the Moon. Apollo 9 and 10 were practice missions for the real thing, which was Apollo 11.

Neil Armstrong and Buzz Aldrin during the Moon landing, 20 July 1969.

THE MOON LANDING

Under the command of Neil Armstrong (1930–2012), the three-man Apollo 11 crew was launched by a Saturn V rocket on July 16, 1969. The Apollo spacecraft had three parts: the Lunar Command Module contained the astronauts' cabin; the Service Module contained supplies and fuel; and the Lunar Lander was for landing on the Moon.

After entering orbit around the Moon, Neil Armstrong and Buzz Aldrin (born 1930) moved into the Lunar Module, leaving Michael Collins (born 1930) to pilot the Command Module. Aldrin landed the Lunar Module on the plain called the Sea of Tranquility. On 21 July, Armstrong was the first to step onto the Moon, saying the famous words: "That's one small step for [a] man, one giant leap for mankind." Armstrong and Aldrin spent 21 hours on the Moon's surface, before rejoining the Command Module and splashing down in the Pacific Ocean.

LUNAR COMMAND MODULE

The Lunar Command module was called "Columbia" and was the living quarters for the three-person crew of the Apollo 11 mission.

PIECES REQUIRED

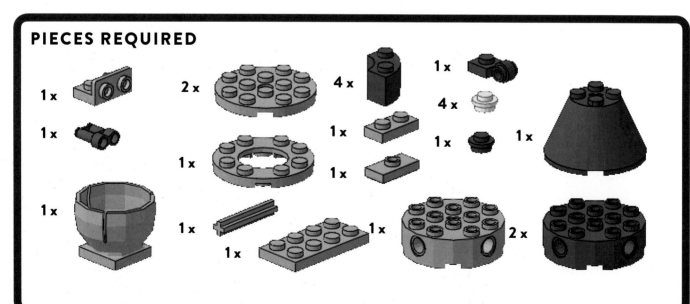

1 x

1 x

1 x

2 x

1 x

1 x

1 x

4 x

1 x

1 x

1 x

4 x

1 x

2 x

1 x

1 x

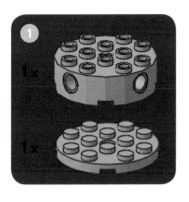

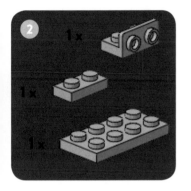

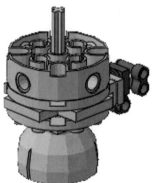

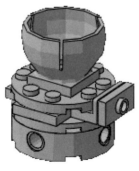
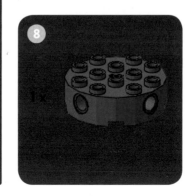

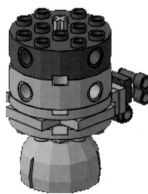

9

4 x

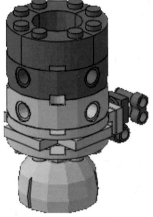

11

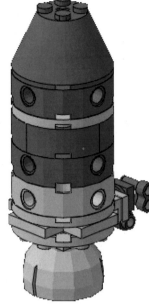

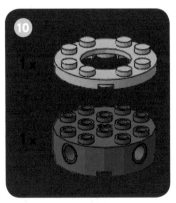

10

1 x

1 x

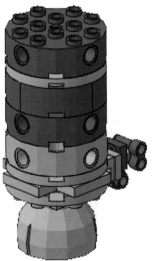

12

4 x

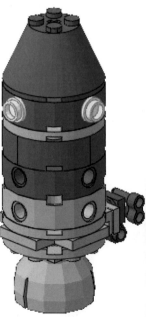

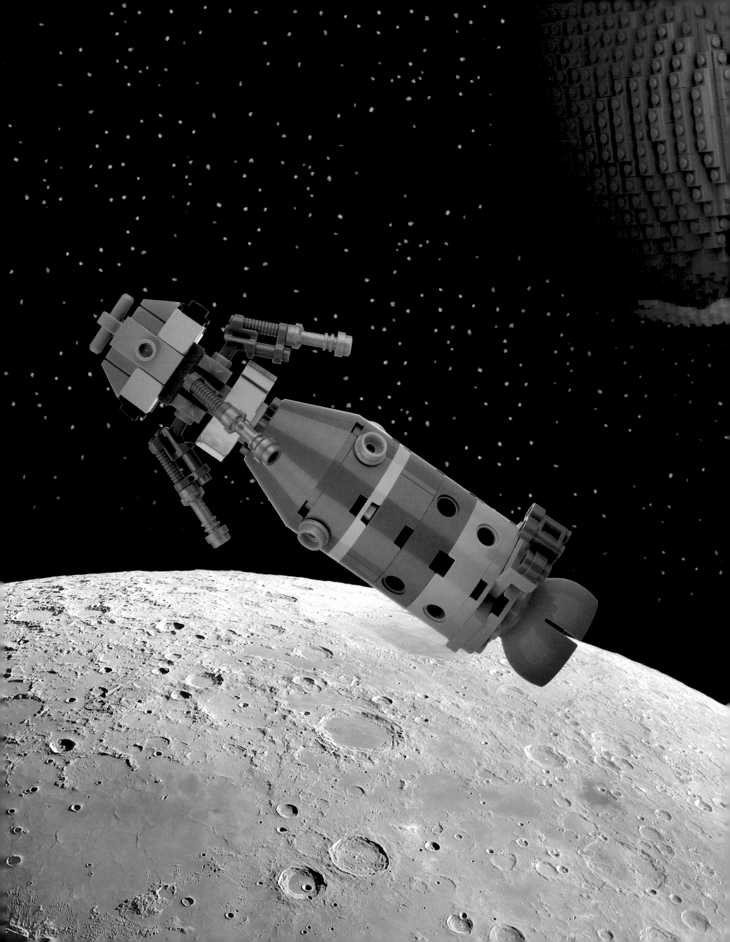

LUNAR LANDER

First launched in 1968, the Lunar Lander was the first manned spacecraft to land on the moon.

 You can fit the builds for the Lunar Command Module and the Lunar Lander together, just like they were in space!

PIECES REQUIRED

1 x   4 x   4 x   1 x 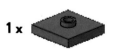   5 x   2 x
4 x

1 x   6 x   2 x   3 x   2 x

1 x   4 x   1 x   2 x    2 x   2 x

1 2 x

2 1 x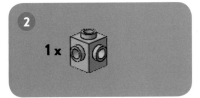

3 2 x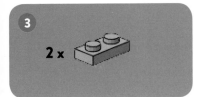

4 2 x 2 x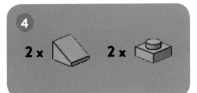

5 1 x 2 x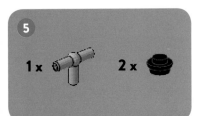

6 1 x 2 x 1 x 2 x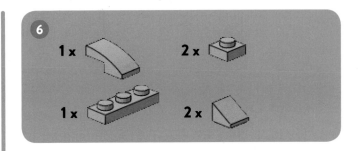

A **B** **C**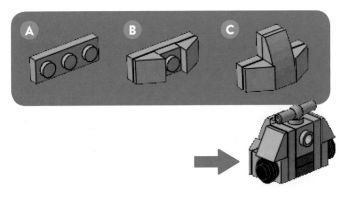

7 1 x 2 x 1 x 1 x 1 x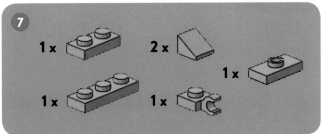

A **B** **C** **D** **E**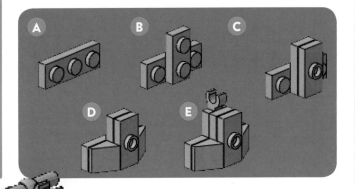

8

2 x 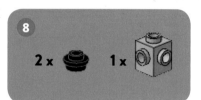　1 x

9

2 x

10

1 x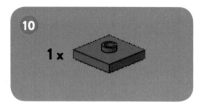

11

4 x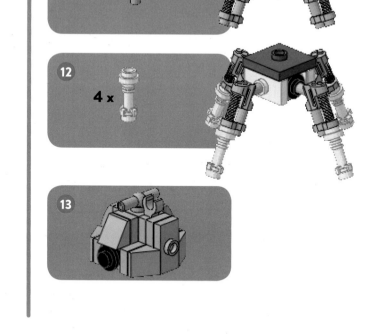

12

4 x

13

14

2 x　　4 x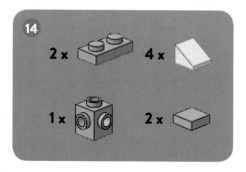

1 x　　2 x

A　　　　**B**

C　　　　**D**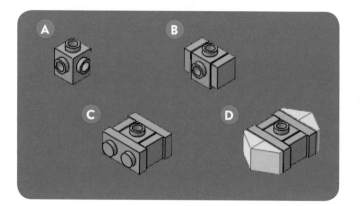

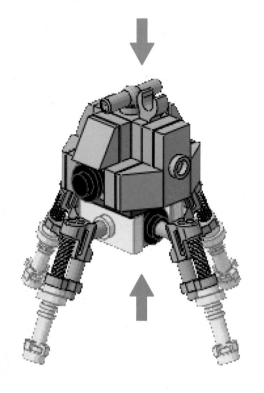

ROCKETS AND SPACE PLANES

A spacecraft is a vehicle that flies in outer space. Spacecraft include manned spacecraft, carrying a human crew; unmanned space probes; and satellites. A spacecraft needs a launch vehicle, often called a rocket. The rocket lifts the spacecraft from the Earth's surface with huge power and speed.

BLAST OFF!

Nearly all spacecraft use an "expendable" rocket to get them off the ground. Expendable rockets are used only once. Rockets get their power from burning fuel. This creates hot gas, which shoots out of the bottom of the rocket. The downward force sends the rocket upward, at over 8 km (5 miles) per second. When a rocket has carried its spacecraft high enough, they separate. The rocket burns up as it plummets back to Earth.

Today's manned spacecraft are in three parts, or modules. The orbital module is where the crew sits for takeoff and during their mission. The service module contains the engines. When the crew has completed their mission, they move into the re-entry module. The orbital and service modules are abandoned and burn up. The re-entry module is slowed by parachutes as it falls back to Earth. It usually lands in a desert.

Lift off for the Apollo 11 mission to the Moon, 16 July 1969.

The space shuttle orbiter Columbia completed its first mission in 1981.

THE SPACE SHUTTLE

The United States' Space Shuttle was first used in 1982. It was different from other spacecraft because it did not need a separate rocket. It was lifted into space by its own rocket boosters. The Space Shuttle was made up of an orbiter vehicle, rocket boosters, and a fuel tank. After launch, the rocket boosters separated from the orbiter and parachuted back to Earth, where they could be re-used. Only the fuel tank was abandoned.

The orbiter was a winged spaceplane. After completing its mission, it flew back to Earth and landed on a runway. Even though the Space Shuttle was mostly reusable, it was very expensive to run. It was also less safe than other spacecraft. It has not been used since 2011.

The space shuttle Challanger launched from the Kennedy Space Centre in 1983. The pilot, Sally Ride, became the first woman to fly in space on this mission.

SOYUZ LIFTER

The Soyuz rocket family are a Russian carrier rocket program, commissioned to launch spacecraft and other payloads into space.

PIECES REQUIRED

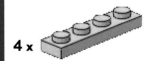 4 x

 18 x

 2 x

 1 x

 4 x

 1 x

1 x

 2 x

 8 x

 1 x

 4 x

 1 x

 1 x

 1 x

 1 x

 4 x

1

1 x   4 x

2

10 x

3

8 x   4 x

4

5 x

5

4 x   1 x

6

1 x   2 x

7

1 x   1 x

8

4 x

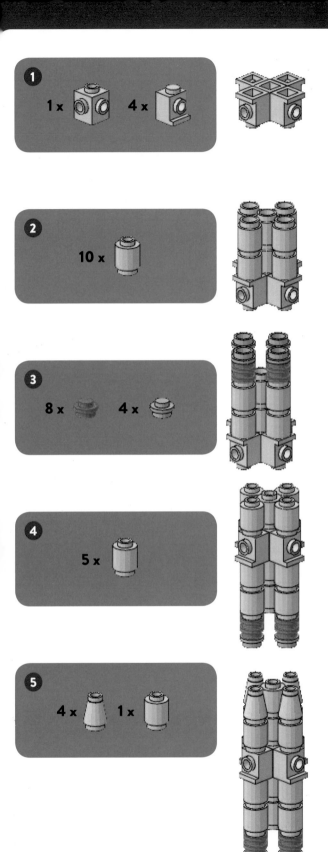

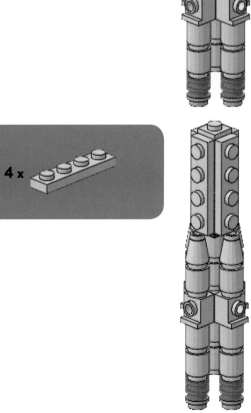

9

2 x

1 x

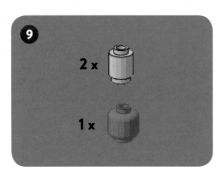

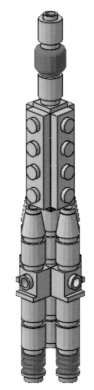

11

1 x

1 x

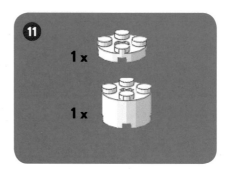

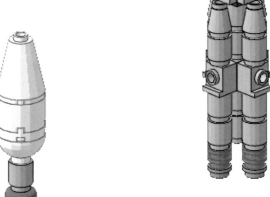

10

1 x

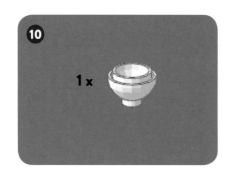

12

1 x

ARIANE ROCKET

The Ariane rocket family are a series of launch vehicles. The first one, Ariane 1, launched in 1979.

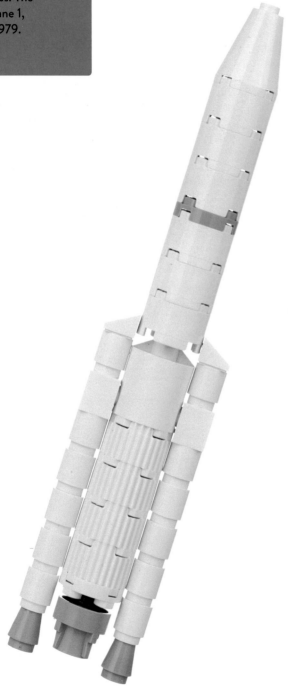

PIECES REQUIRED

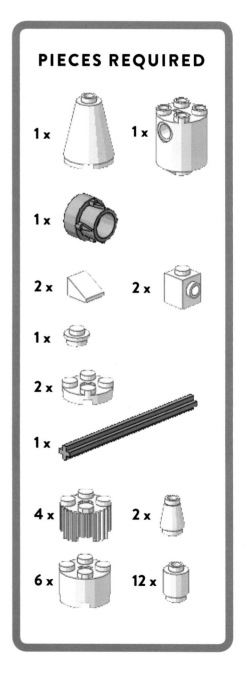

1 x   1 x

1 x

2 x   2 x

1 x

2 x

1 x

4 x   2 x

6 x   12 x

1

1 x 1 x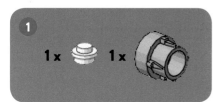

2

1 x 1 x

3

2 x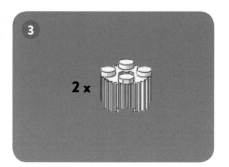

4

1 x 1 x

5

2 x 2 x 2 x 12 x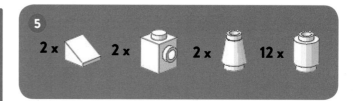

A   B   C   D

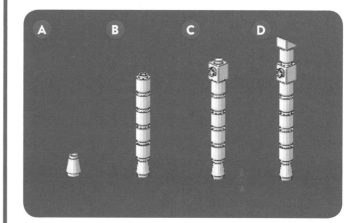

make **2**

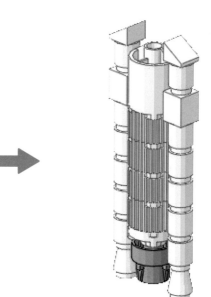

6

1 x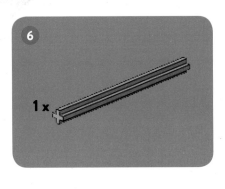

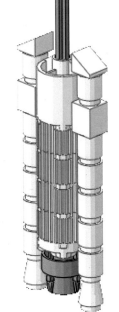

8

3 x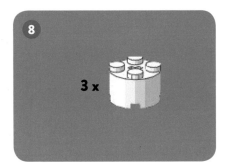

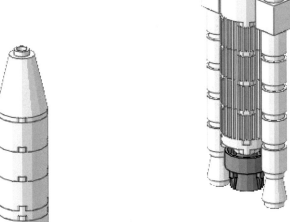

7

1 x **2 x**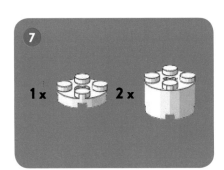

9

1 x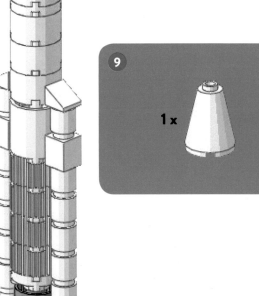

VOSTOK 1 ROCKET

The Vostok 1 rocket carried Soviet cosmonaut Yuri Gagarin into space.

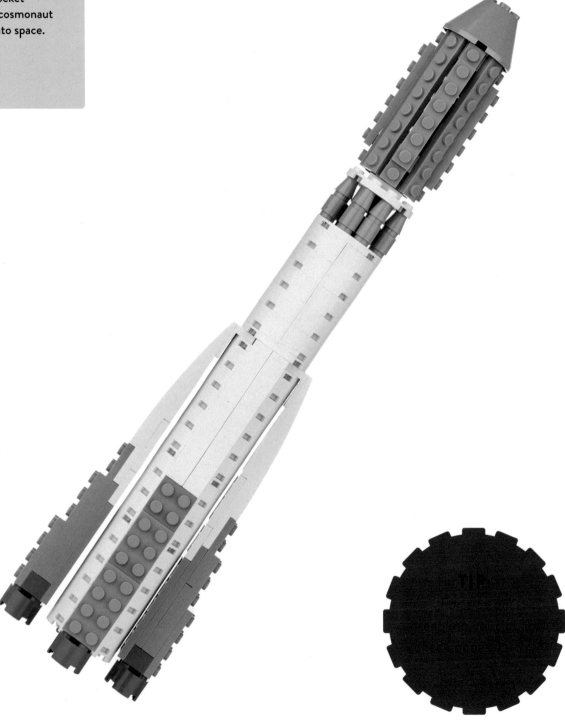

PIECES REQUIRED

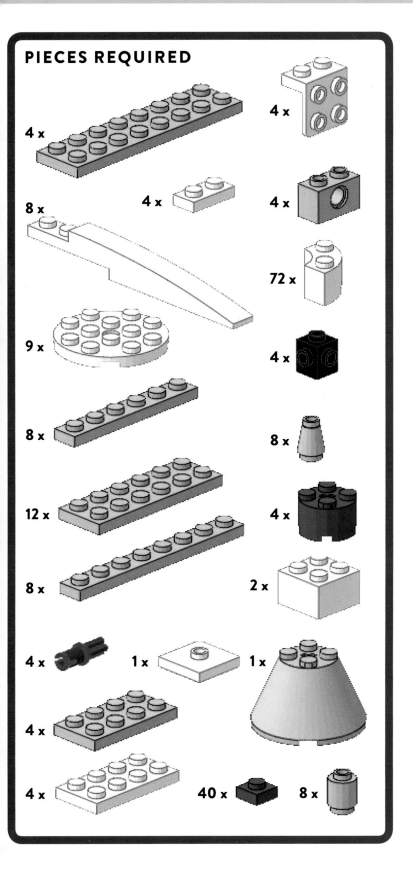

4 x

8 x

9 x

8 x

12 x

8 x

4 x   1 x   1 x

4 x

4 x

40 x   8 x

4 x

4 x

4 x

72 x

4 x

8 x

4 x

2 x

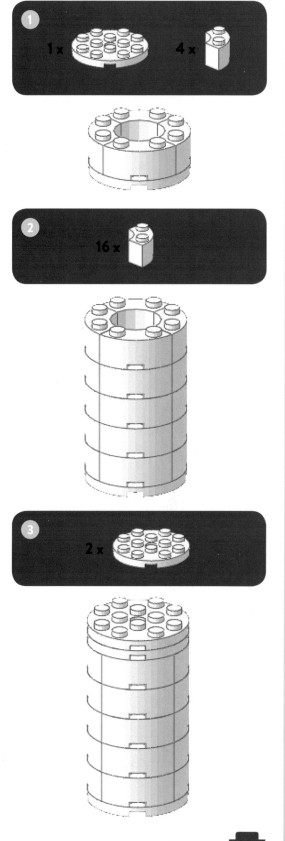

1   1 x   4 x

2   16 x

3   2 x

12 x

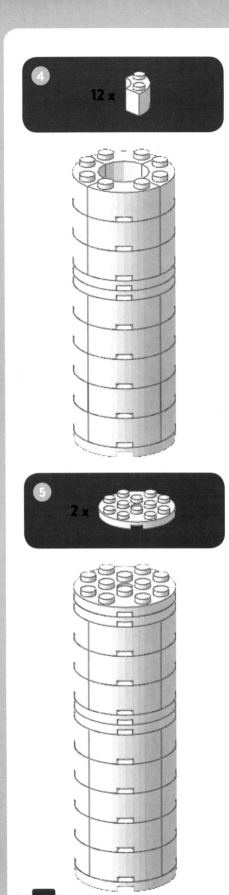

5

2 x

6

1 x

20 x

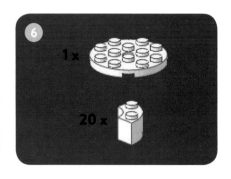
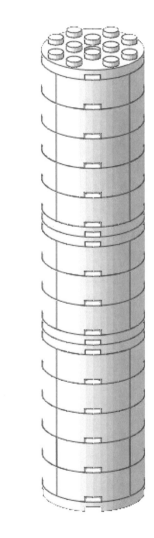

4 x

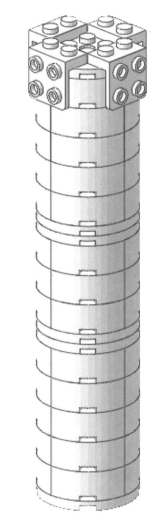

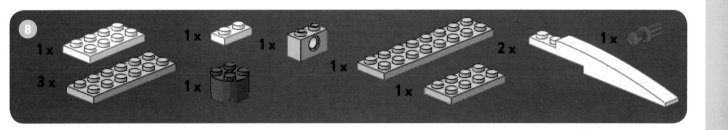

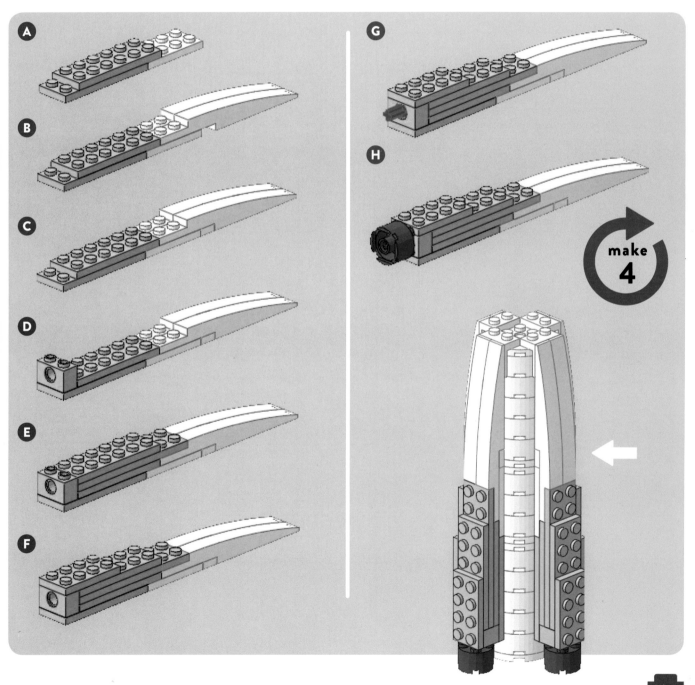

make
4

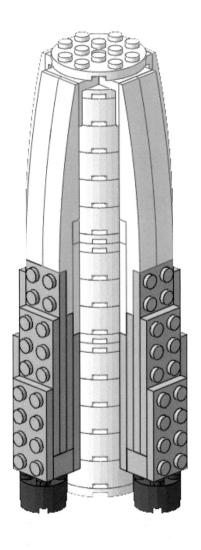

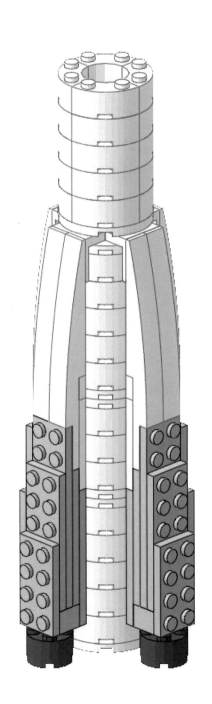

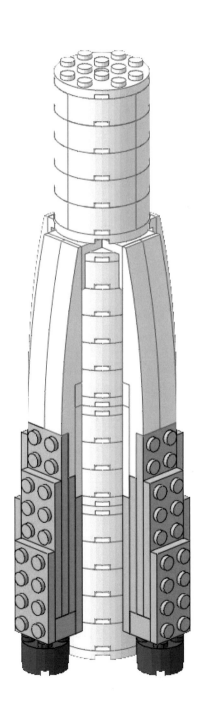

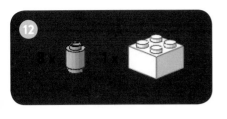

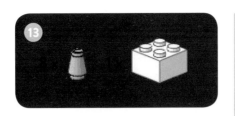

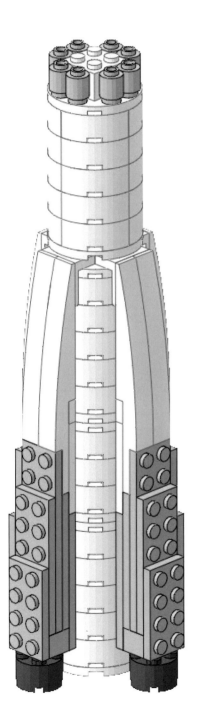

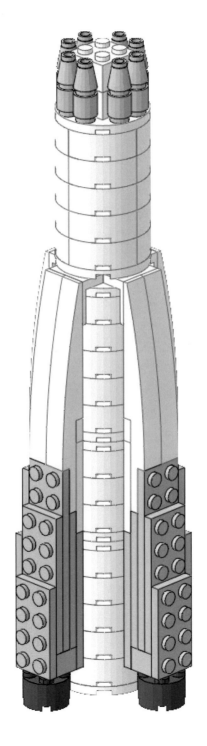

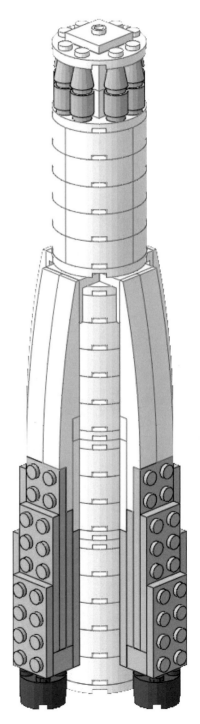

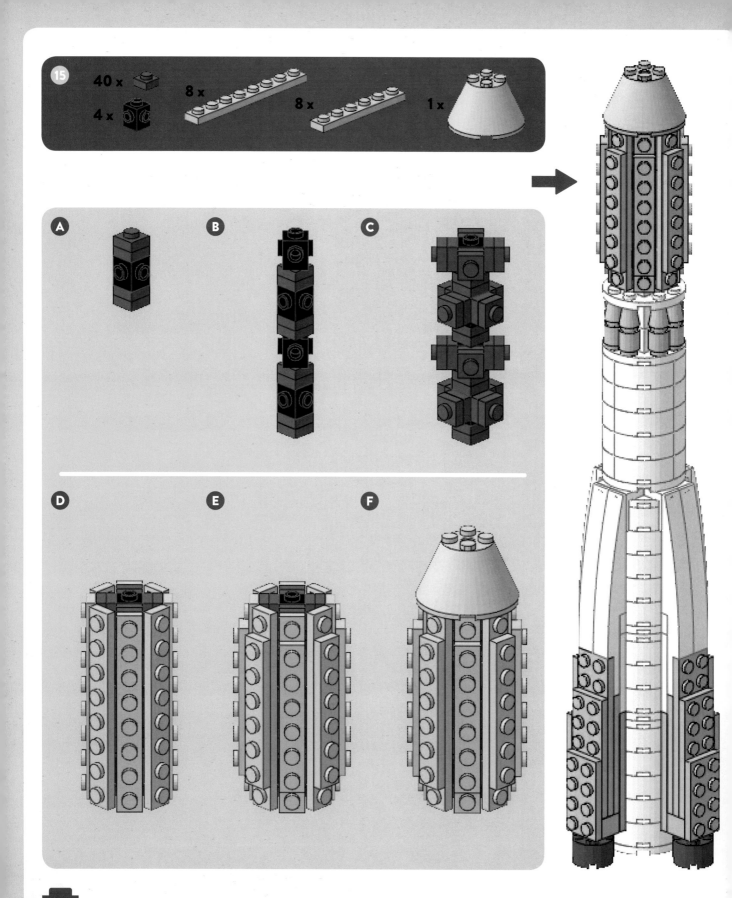

SATURN V ROCKET

The Saturn V Rocket was first launched in 1967. It was later used to launch Skylab, the first American space station, in 1973.

PIECES REQUIRED

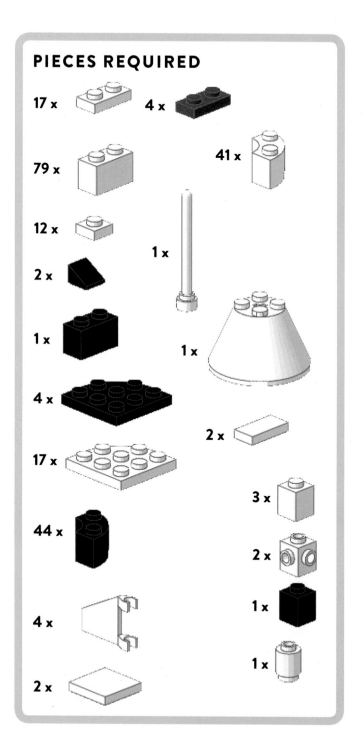

17 x

4 x

79 x

41 x

12 x

1 x

2 x

1 x

1 x

4 x

1 x

2 x

17 x

3 x

2 x

44 x

1 x

4 x

1 x

2 x

PIECES REQUIRED CONTINUED

4 x

2 x

3 x

1 x

2 x

8 x

3 x

5 x

6 x

2 x

6 x

1 x

3 x

2 x

1 x

1 x

1 x

3 x

5 x

1 x

3 x

2 x

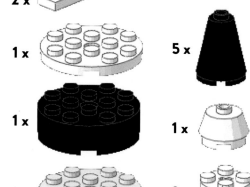

1

4 x

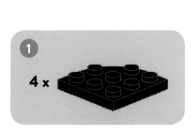

4

5x

2

1 x

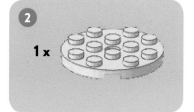

5

5x

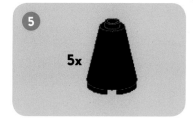

3

4 x

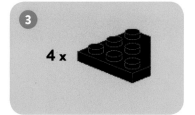

6

4 x

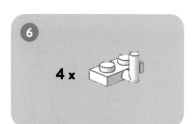

7

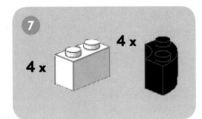

4 x

4 x

8

4 x

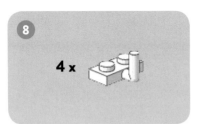

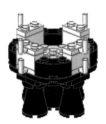

9

4 x

4 x

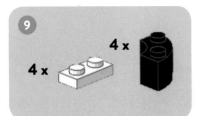

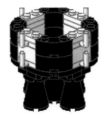

10

4 x

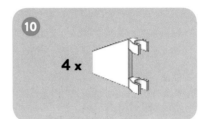

11

4 x

4 x

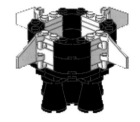

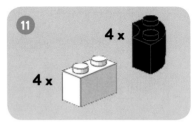

12

12 x

12 x

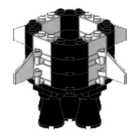

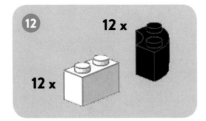

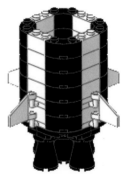

13

4 x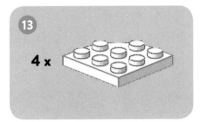

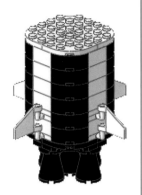

14

12 x

13 x

1 x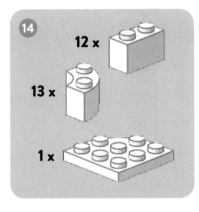

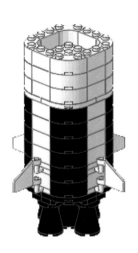

15

4 x

4 x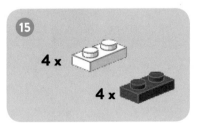

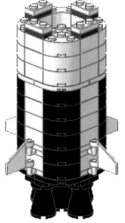

16

4 x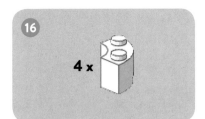

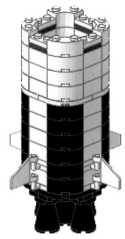

17

3 x

2 x 3 x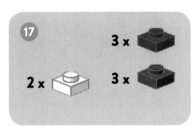

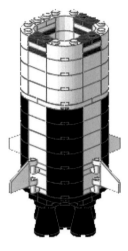

18

4 x

4 x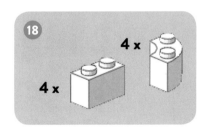

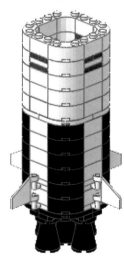

19

4 x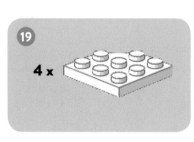

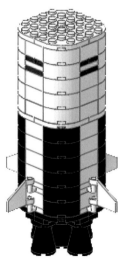

20

8 x 8 x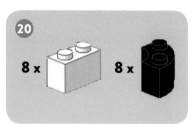

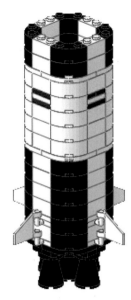

21

12 x 12 x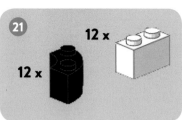

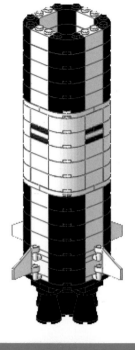

22

4 x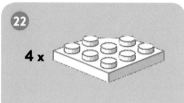

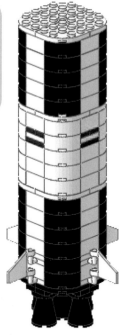

23

12 x 12 x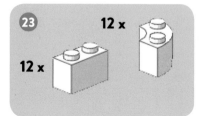

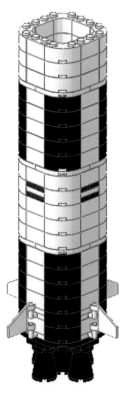

24

8 x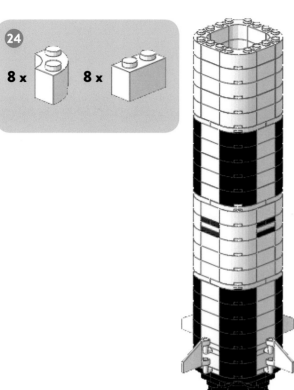

8 x

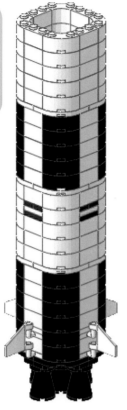

26

2 x

2 x

2 x

1 x

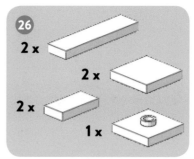

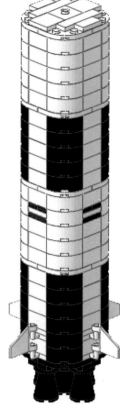

25

4 x

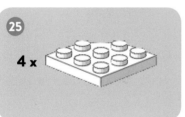

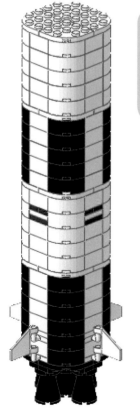

27

2 x

1 x

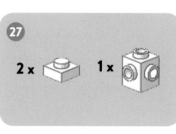

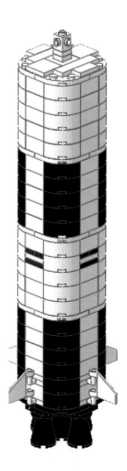

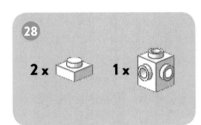

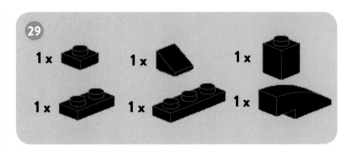

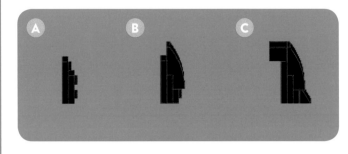

A   B   C

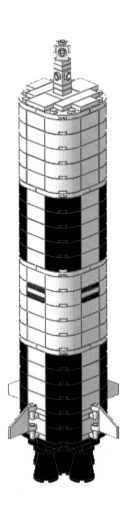

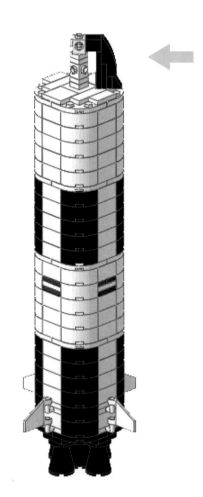

30

3 x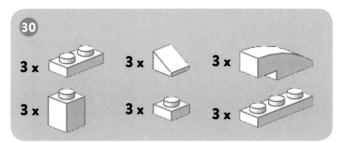
3 x
3 x
3 x
3 x
3 x

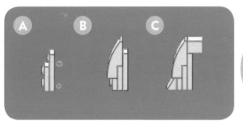

A B C

make
3

1 x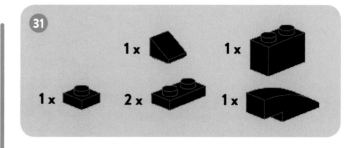
1 x
1 x
2 x
1 x

A B C

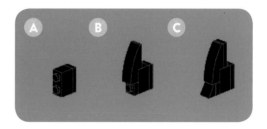

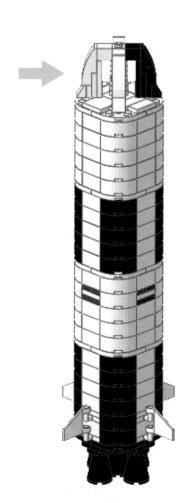

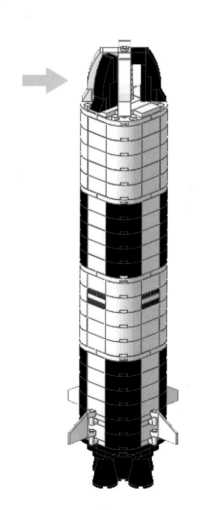

32

3 x 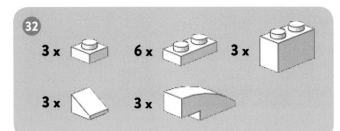 6 x 3 x

3 x 3 x

A B C

make **3**

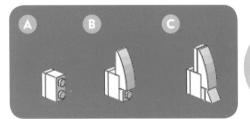

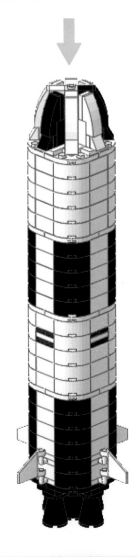

33

2 x 1 x

1 x

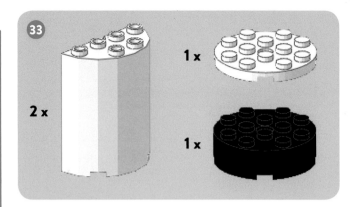

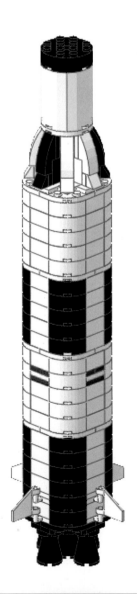

34

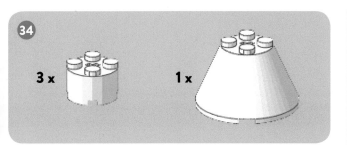

3 x   1 x

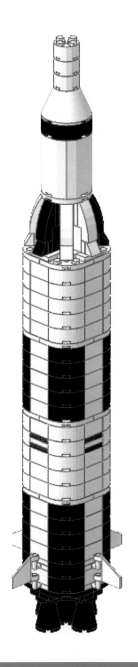

35

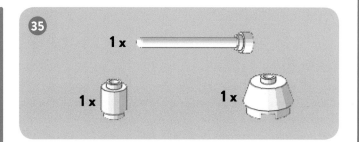

1 x

1 x   1 x

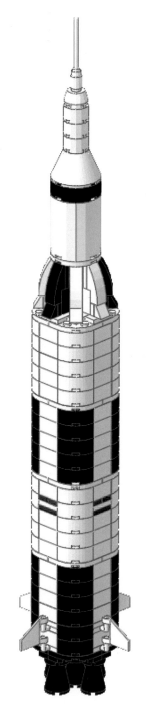

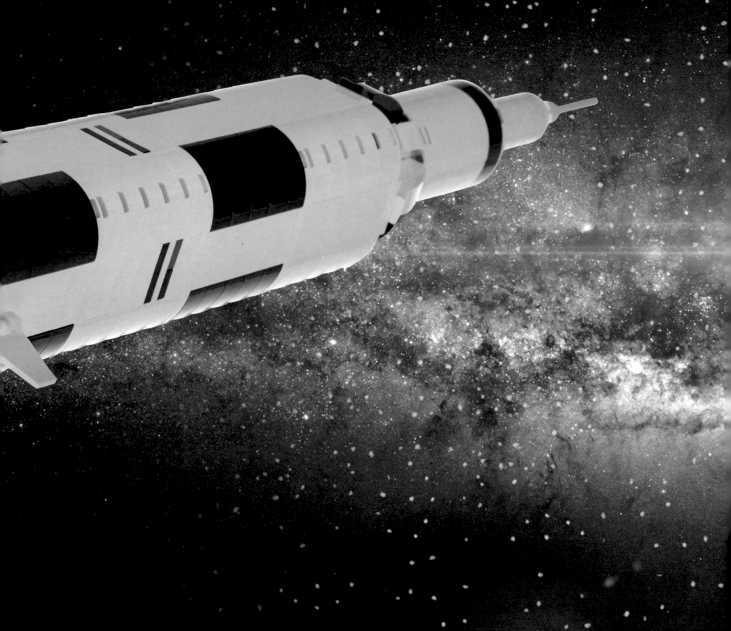

LONG MARCH ROCKET

Also called the Changzheng rocket, these expendable launch systems are operated by China, and used as launch vehicles.

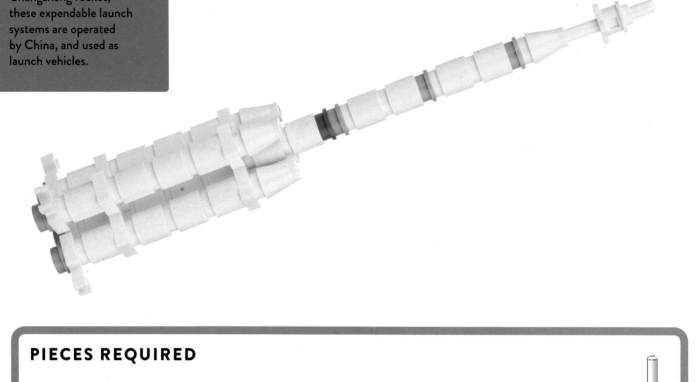

PIECES REQUIRED

4 x   1 x   2 x   26 x   8 x   5 x   1 x

1

5 x

1 x

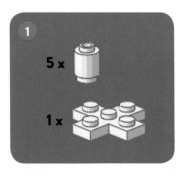

2

4 x

3

4 x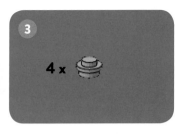

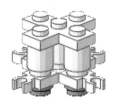

4

5 x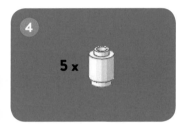

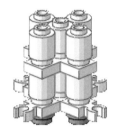

5

10 x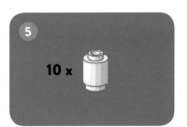

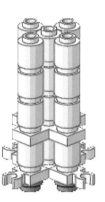

6

1 x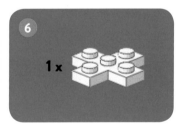

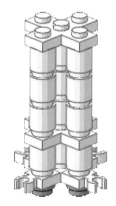

7

1 x 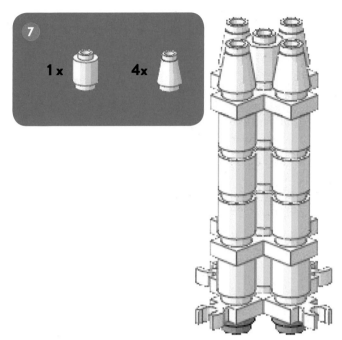 4x

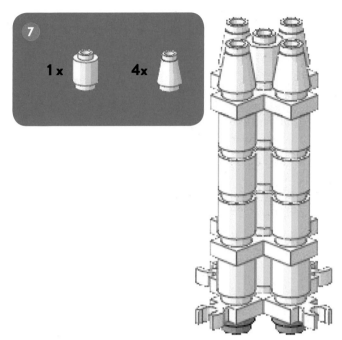

8

2 x  2 x

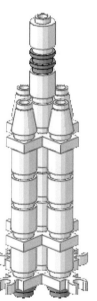

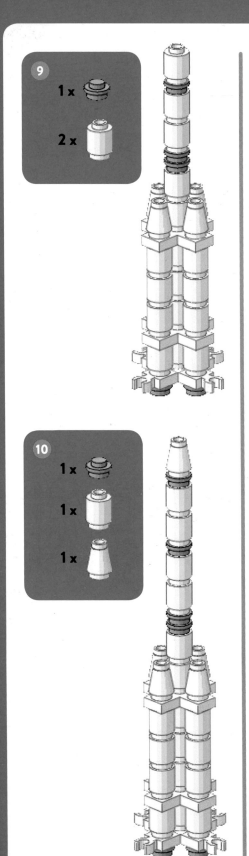

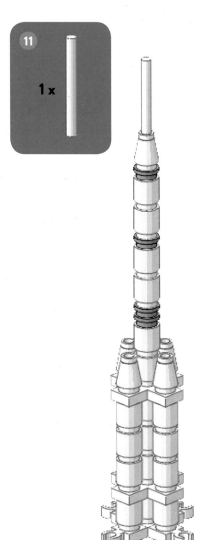

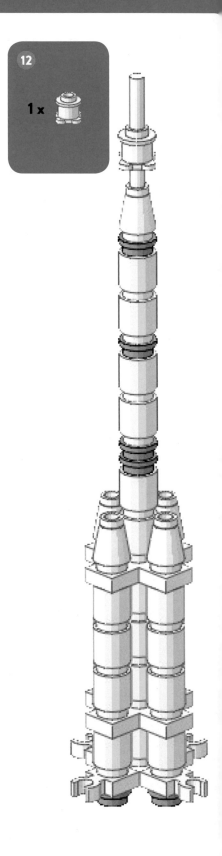

DELTA IV ROCKET

The Delta IV launch vehicle is still in active use, and has been a part of many classified missions for the US military.

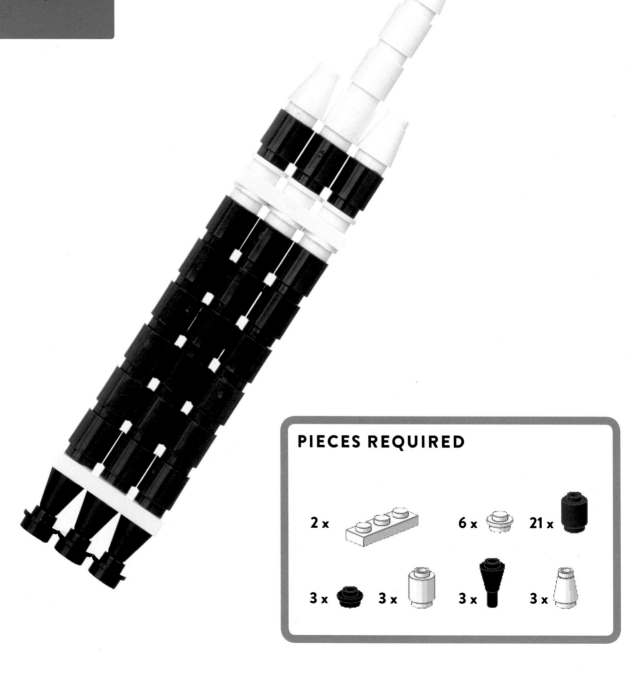

PIECES REQUIRED

2 x

6 x

21 x

3 x

3 x

3 x

3 x

1

1 x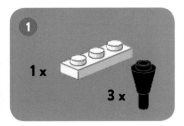

3 x

2

3 x

3

3 x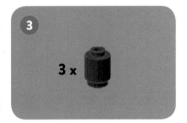

4

15 x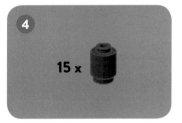

5

3 x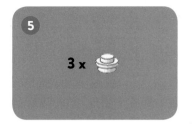

FACT

- Delta IV rockets are launched from Cape Canaveral, Florida, and Vandenberg Air Force Base, California, to carry satellites into Earth orbit. The first Delta IV lifted off in 2002.

- The Delta IV Heavy is the largest version of the Delta IV. It can carry a cargo weighing 28,790 kg (63,470 lbs) into low Earth orbit – that's the equivalent of carrying more than 400 adult humans.

6

1 x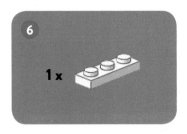

7

3 x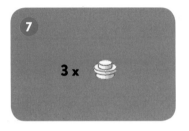

8

3 x

9

1 x 2 x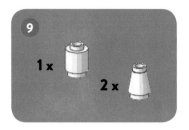

10

2 x 1 x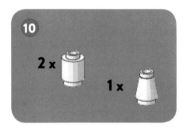

SHUTTLE ORBITER

PIECES REQUIRED

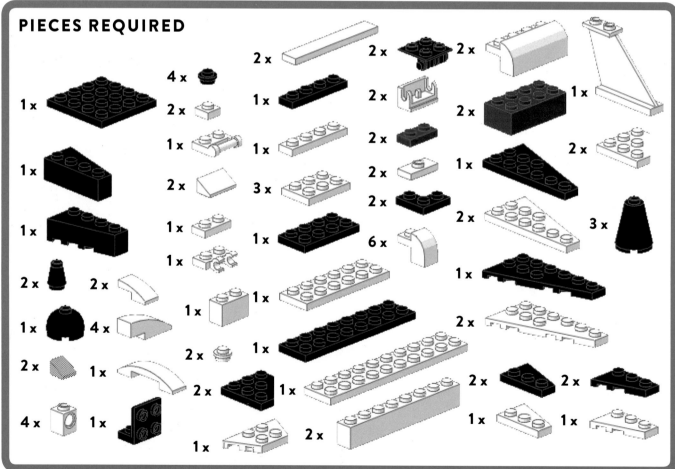

1 x   4 x   2 x   2 x   2 x   2 x

1 x   2 x   1 x   2 x   2 x   1 x

1 x   1 x   1 x   2 x   2 x   2 x

1 x   2 x   3 x   2 x   1 x

1 x   2 x   2 x   3 x

2 x   2 x   1 x   1 x   6 x   1 x

1 x   4 x   1 x   2 x

2 x   1 x   2 x   1 x   2 x   2 x

4 x   1 x   2 x   1 x   1 x   1 x

1 x   2 x

1

1 x
1 x
1 x

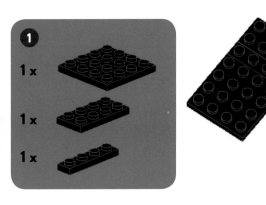

2

1 x

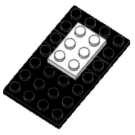

3

1 x

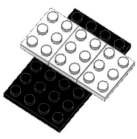

4

1 x
1 x

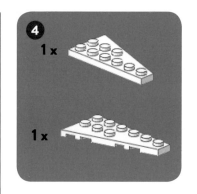

5

1 x
1 x
1 x

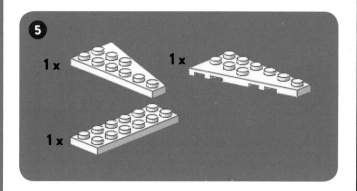

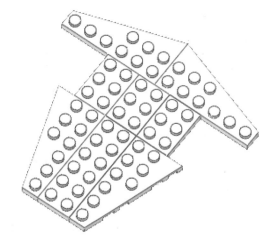

6

2 x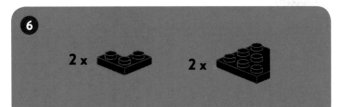

7

2 x

8

1 x 1 x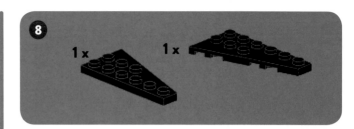

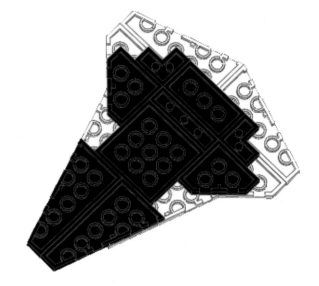

9

2 x 2 x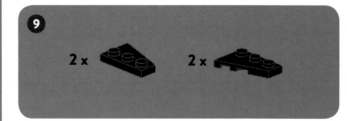

10

1 x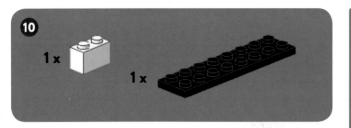

12

1 x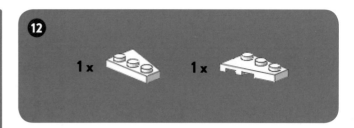

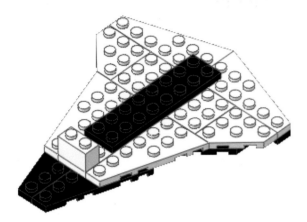

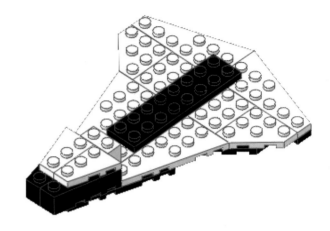

11

1 x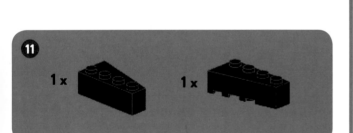

13

2 x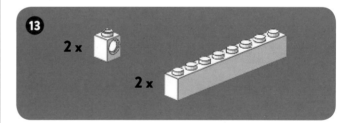

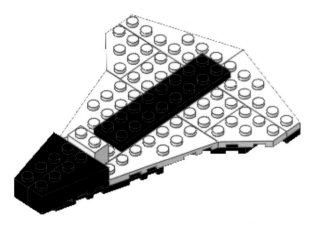

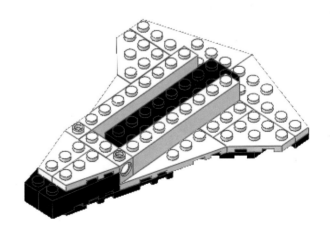

14

2 x 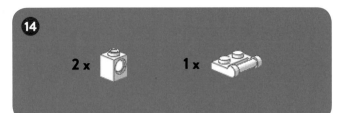 1 x

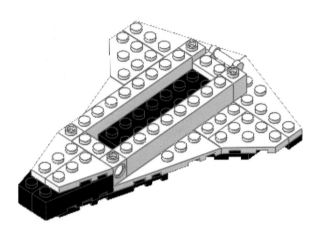

15

4 x

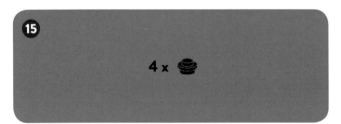

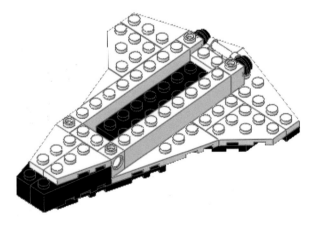

16

2 x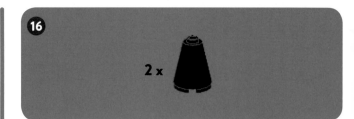

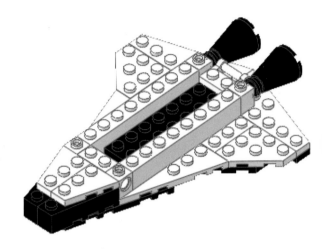

FACT

- The Space Shuttle Orbiter is 37 metres long, and weighs 5990 kilograms. That's as nearly as long as four double decker buses and as heavy as 14 African elephants!

- There were five different orbiters: Columbia, Challenger, Discovery, Atlantis, and Endeavour. The last space shuttle orbiter mission (using Atlantis) was in July 2011.

17

1 x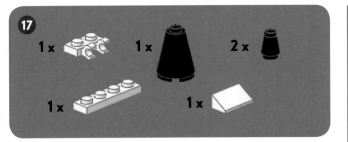
1 x
2 x
1 x
1 x

A
C

B
D

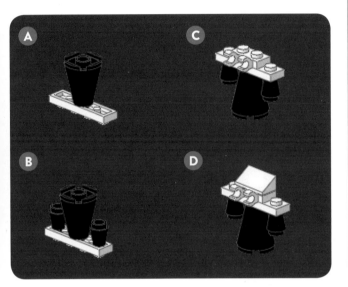

18

1 x
2 x

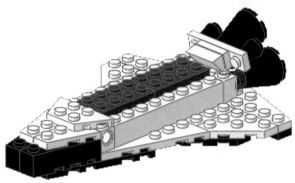

19

1 x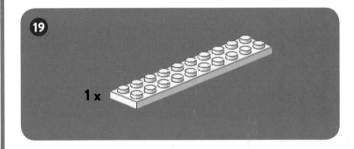

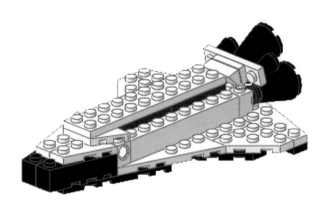

20

2 x

2 x

21

6 x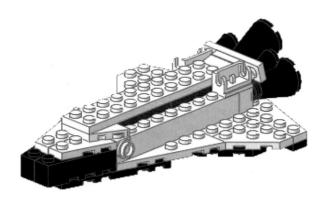

2 x

1 x

22

2 x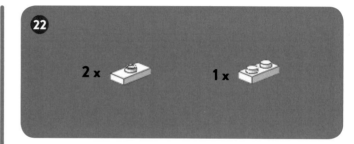

1 x

23

2 x

1 x

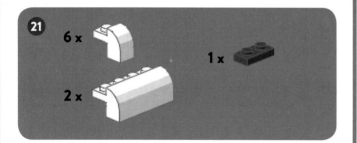

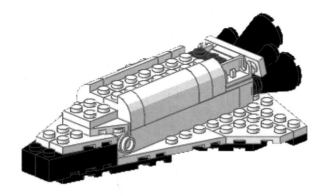

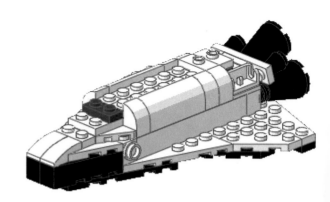

24

2 x 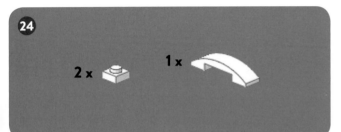 1 x

25

1 x 2 x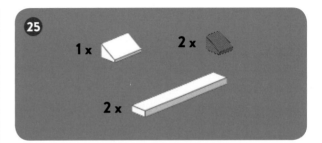

2 x

FACT

- The Space Shuttle Orbiter can usually carry up to seven crew members.

- The Space Shuttle Orbiter had three sets of landing gear, that would deploy downwards through the heat shield. These could only be deployed manually, as it would have been a disaster to have them open early!

26

1 x

2 x

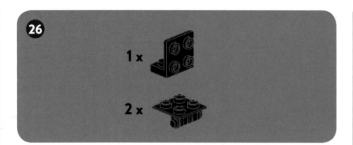

27

4 x

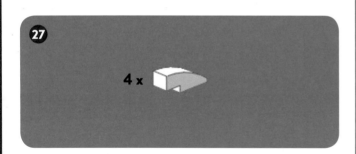

28

1 x

1 x

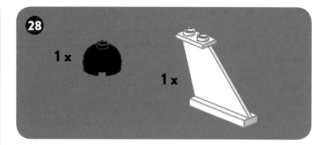

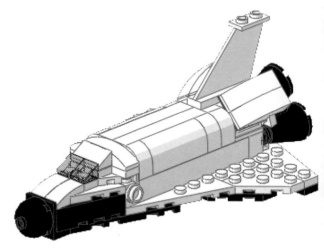

HUMANS LIVING IN SPACE

A space station is a spacecraft designed to remain in orbit around the Earth for a long period of time. It has facilities for crew to live and work, and docks for other spacecraft to arrive with crew and supplies. In 2016, there are two space stations in orbit: the International Space Station (ISS) and the Chinese station Tiangong-1.

CHANGING SPACE STATIONS

The world's first space station, Salyut 1, was launched by the Soviet Union in 1971. Unlike today's stations, it was launched in one piece rather than built in space from ready-made modules. It was just 20 metres (65 ft) long and 4 metres (13 ft) wide, with two cramped compartments for crew and equipment. It was lived in for 23 days, and lasted in orbit for 175 days.

From 1973 to 1979, NASA's first space station, Skylab, orbited Earth. The station was damaged during its unmanned launch. Luckily, when its crew arrived, they carried out the first ever in-space repair. From 1986, the Soviet space station Mir was the first to be assembled in orbit, over ten years. When complete, it was 19 metres (62 ft) long and 28 metres (90 ft) wide. Mir was in orbit for 15 years and, later in its life, was the first station to house an international crew.

NASA's Atlantis shuttle and the Earth as seen from Mir, July 1995.

WHAT ARE SPACE STATIONS USED FOR?

Space stations are laboratories and observatories, with equipment for carrying out experiments and studying the Solar System. As a space station spins round Earth, astronauts experience weightlessness. This means that they float, appearing to be unaffected by the force of gravity. On a space station, astronauts can study the effects of weightlessness on the human body. This knowledge will be useful when planning spaceflights to distant worlds in the future.

Weightlessness is a perfect environment for carrying out experiments and research without gravity affecting the results. For example, scientists on board the ISS managed to construct "micro-balloons" that can contain cancer-fighting drugs. No one had managed to construct the minuscule balloons on Earth. The balloons help doctors target cancerous cells without damaging healthy ones.

Eileen M. Collins at the pilot's station prior to a rendezvous with Mir. Missions like this paved the way for successful missions between the space shuttles and the ISS.

THE INTERNATIONAL SPACE STATION

Orbiting 390 km (240 miles) above our heads is a giant laboratory where astronauts work in space, living for months without the pull of gravity. Construction on the International Space Station (ISS) began in 1998 and is the work of five space agencies, representing 16 nations. By the time it was completed in 2011, it was as big as an American football field.

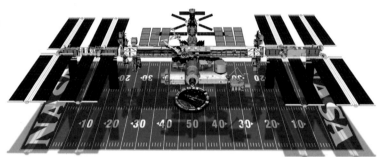

HOW TO GET TO THE INTERNATIONAL SPACE STATION

Getting to the International Space Station used to take two days, but now you can get from Earth to the ISS in four orbits – that's only six hours! The only way to get to the ISS is on a Soyuz rocket, a Russian space vehicle. It launches from a special space launch facility in Baikonur, Kazakhstan.

The ISS flies at an altitude of 354 km (220 miles) – 40 times the height of Mount Everest! – and is always travelling at about 28,163 km/h (17,500 mph).

Because of this, before astronauts can get on board, they have to chase it down, and pull up along the side! After catching up to the ISS, the shuttle turns and flips over, lining up with the docking station. The docking procedure is slow and has to be done very carefully. A computer controls this, but crew members monitor the process very closely, and can take over if they need to.

Once they are locked together, it takes half an hour to equalize the pressure and finally open the hatch. Only then can the current ISS residents and the new astronauts finally meet each other!

NASA astronaut Scott Kelly and ESA astronaut Tim Peake shared this incredible photograph of aurora borealis taken from the International Space Station on 20 January 2016.

ISS

SIZE: 109 x 73 metres
(356 x 240 ft)

WEIGHT: 450 tonnes

COST: 150 billion dollars

CREW: Up to 10 people

More than an acre of solar panels provide the power and energy for the ISS. These solar panels make it the brightest object in the night sky, next to the moon!

WHAT'S ON THE INTERNATIONAL SPACE STATION?

Inside the ISS there are the living quarters (including a gym), laboratories, storage units, and all of the parts of the Space Station that keep everything working.

So what do Astronauts actually do on the ISS? The ISS is a microgravity and space environment research lab. The astronauts who live there conduct experiments in lots of different fields including biology, human biology, physics, astronomy, meteorology, and much more. The astronauts in the ISS can test equipment for other missions, they have grown plants and vegetables in space and they are constantly fixing and maintaining the space station itself. They also take part in medical experiments to see how their bodies are adjusting to living in microgravity for long periods of time.

This zinnia flower is the first flower grown in space. It was grown in the International Space Station's vegetable growing facility.

ISS

The ISS has been visited by astronauts and cosmonauts from 15 different nations. Truly international!

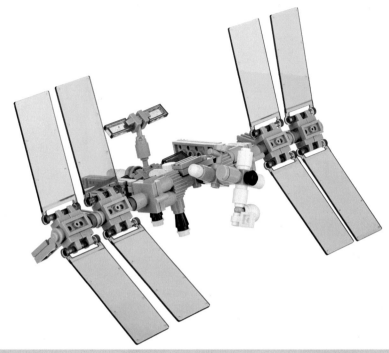

PIECES REQUIRED

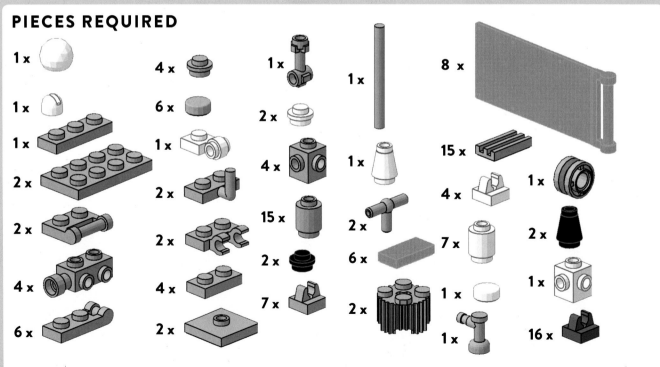

1 x
1 x
1 x
2 x
2 x
4 x
6 x

4 x
6 x
1 x
2 x
2 x
4 x
2 x

1 x
2 x
4 x
15 x
2 x
7 x

1 x
1 x
2 x
6 x
2 x

8 x
15 x
4 x
7 x
1 x
1 x

1 x
1 x
2 x
1 x
16 x

1

1 x  1 x

2

1 x 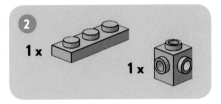 1 x

3

1 x 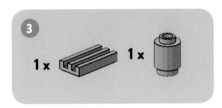 1 x

4

1 x 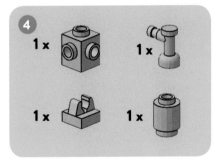 1 x

1 x 1 x

5

1 x 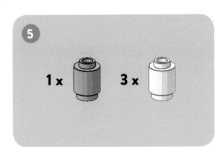 3 x

6

1 x 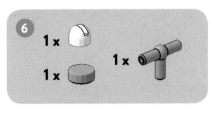 1 x

1 x

7

1 x  1 x

1 x 1 x

8

1 x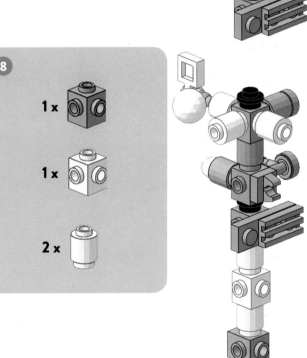

1 x

2 x

9

1 x

1 x

1 x

2 x

1 x

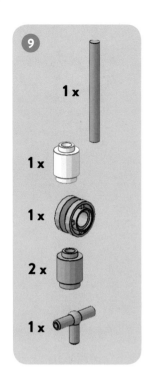
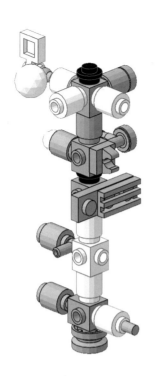

10

2 x

1 x

1 x

1 x

2 x

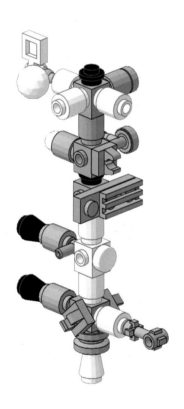

11

2 x

1 x

4 x

2 x

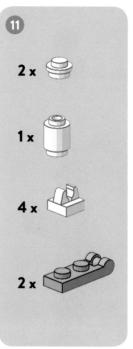
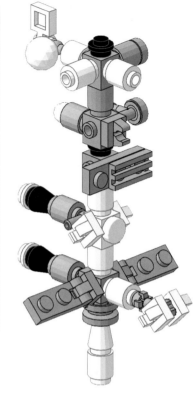

12

6 x

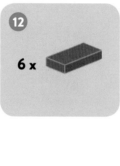
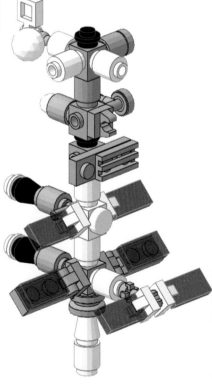

13

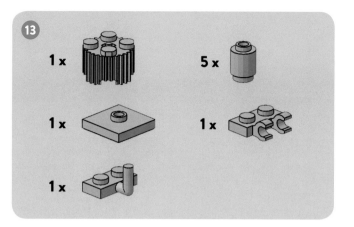

1 x   5 x

1 x   1 x

1 x

FACT

- It took 136 space flights to build the ISS. There are over 8 miles of wires used just to connect the electrical system, and it has two bathrooms and a gym!

- The ISS has a 16.75-metre (55-ft) long robot arm, used mainly for performing assembly and maintenance. This arm is capable of lifting 99,790 kg (220,000 lbs), which is the weight of a space shuttle orbiter.

A

B

C

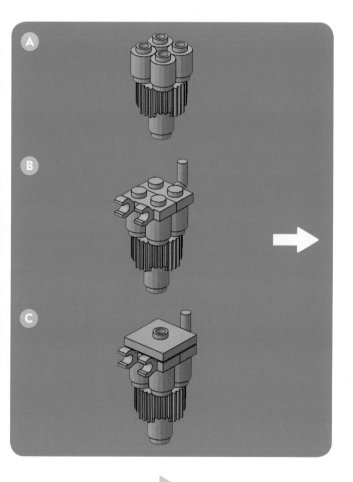

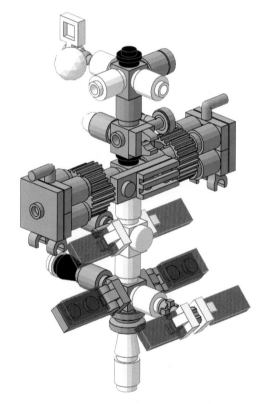

make
2

14

1 x 1 x 5 x

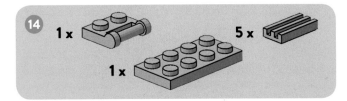

A
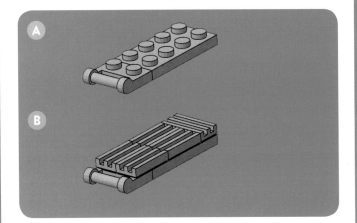
B

make 2

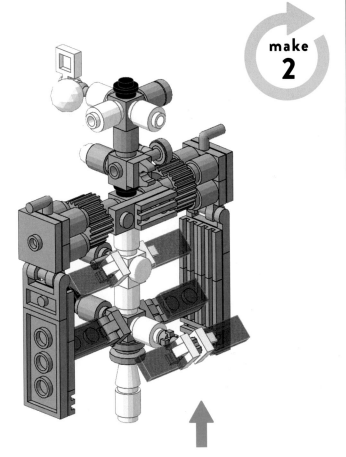

15

1 x 4 x 1 x
1 x 1 x
1 x
2 x
1 x

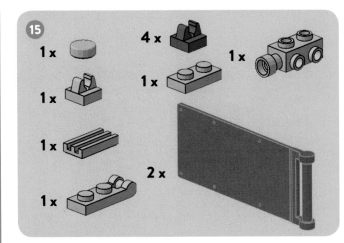

A C
B D
E

make 4

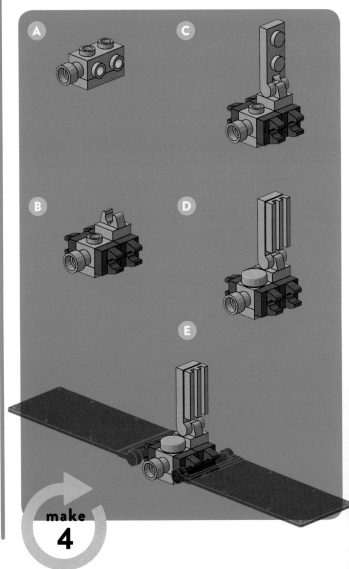

2 x

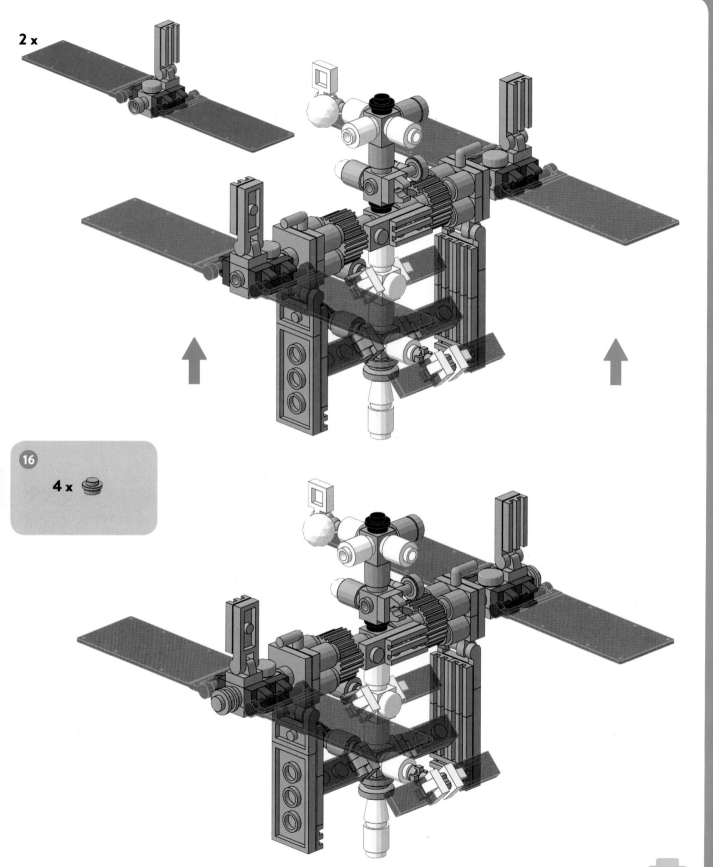

16

4 x 🔘

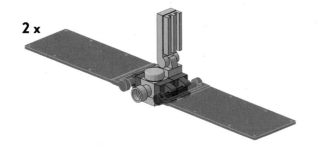

2 x

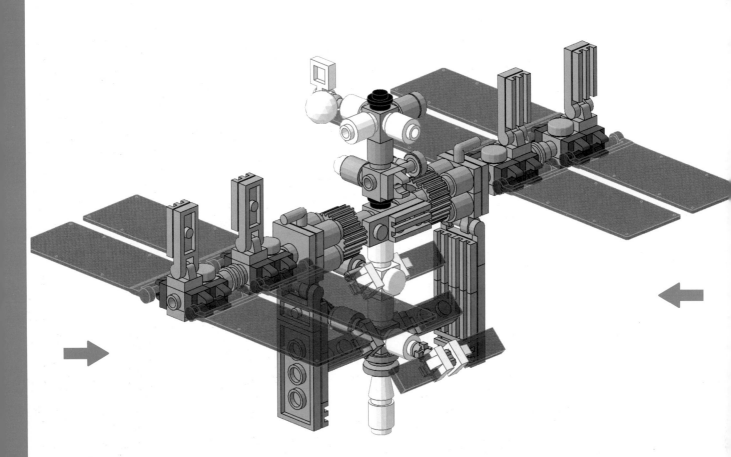

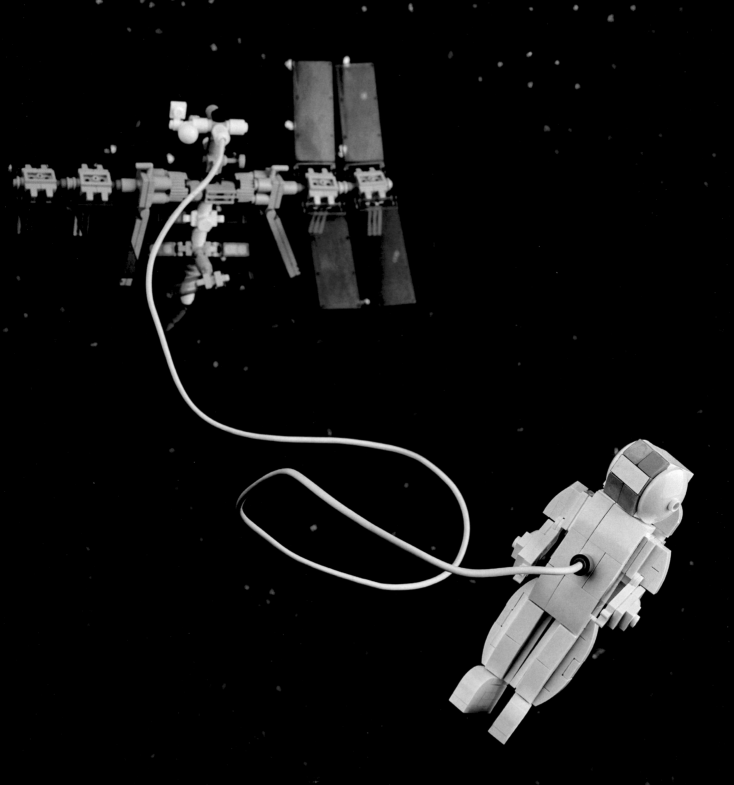

MIR

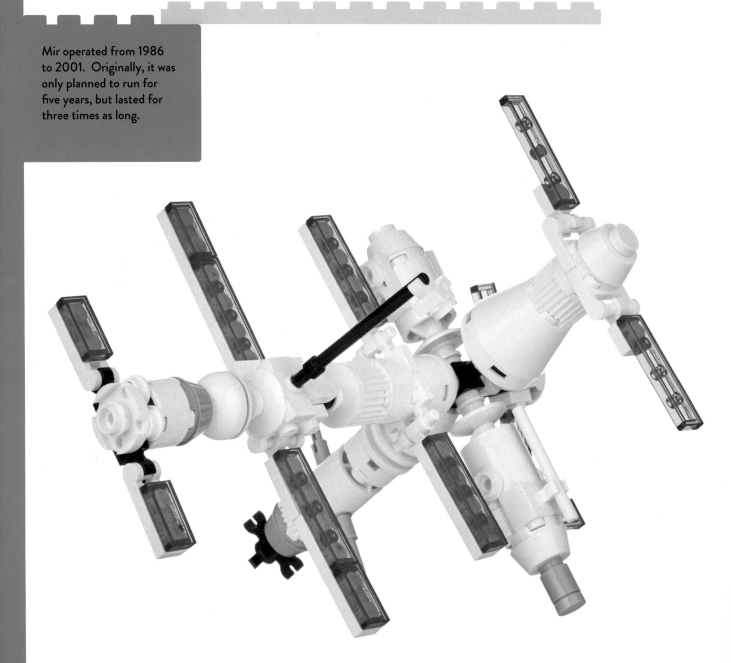

PIECES REQUIRED

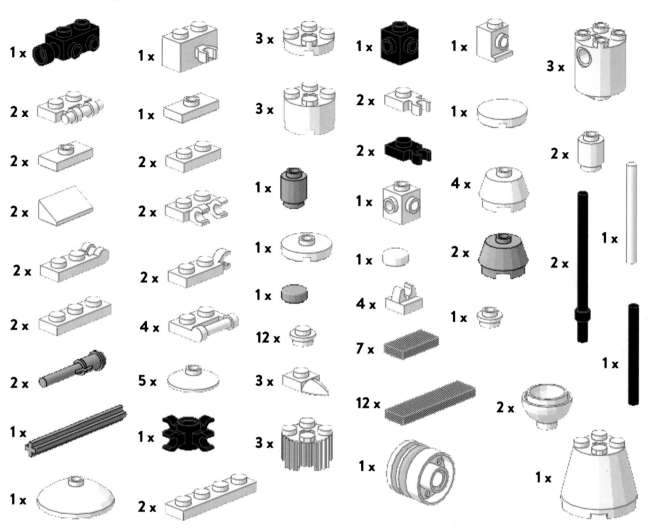

1 x 2 x 2 x 2 x 2 x 2 x 2 x 1 x 1 x

1 x 1 x 2 x 2 x 2 x 2 x 4 x 5 x 1 x 2 x

3 x 3 x 1 x 1 x 1 x 12 x 3 x 3 x

1 x 2 x 2 x 4 x 1 x 1 x 4 x 7 x 12 x 1 x

1 x 1 x 3 x

3 x 2 x 2 x 2 x 1 x 2 x 4 x 2 x 1 x 2 x

1 x 1 x 1 x

FACT

- It took 10 years to assemble the MIR space
  station in orbit, from 1986 to 1996. When
  complete, it was the largest artificial satellite
  in Earth's orbit, until it was succeeded by the
  International Space Station in 2001.

1

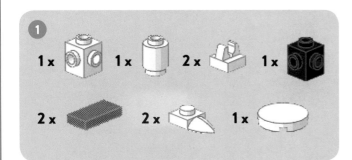

1 x   1 x   2 x   1 x

2 x   2 x   1 x

2

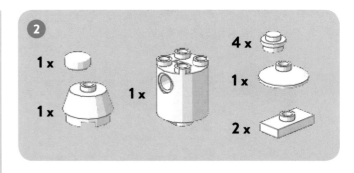

1 x   1 x   4 x

1 x   1 x

2 x

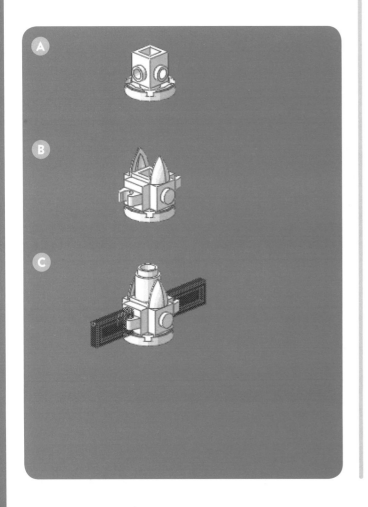

A

B

C

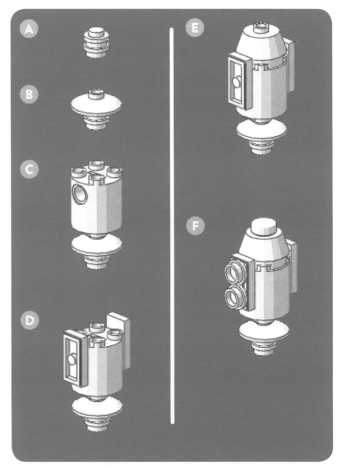

A   E

B

C   F

D

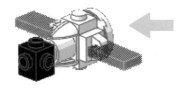

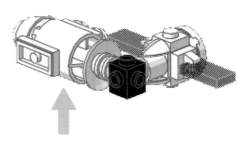

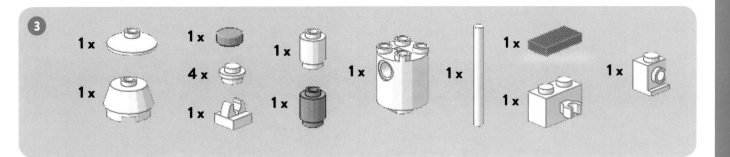

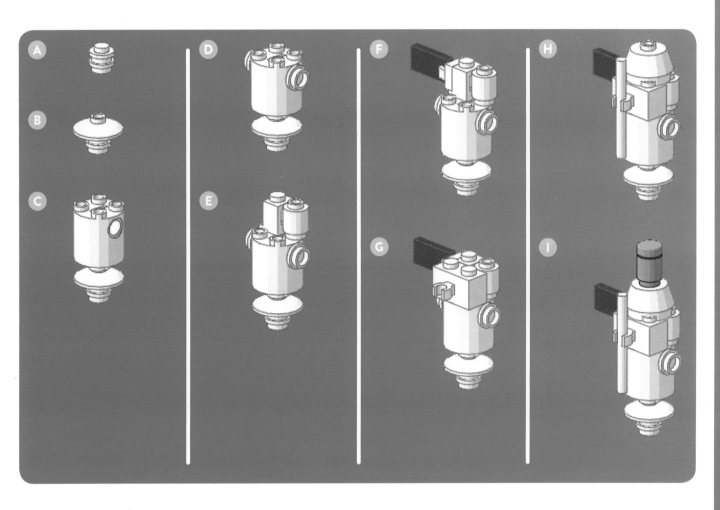

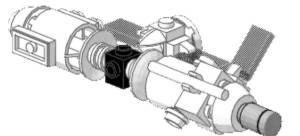

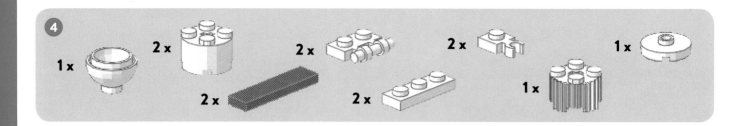

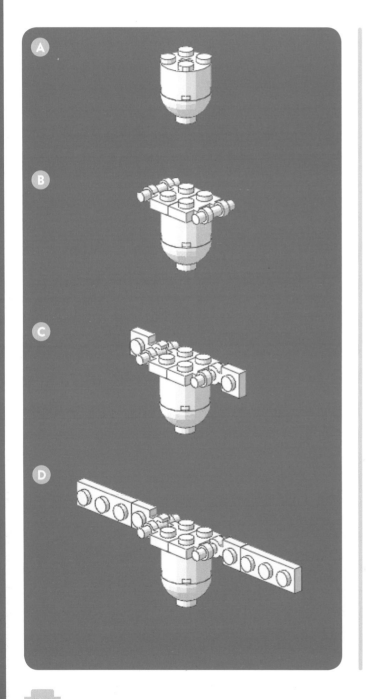

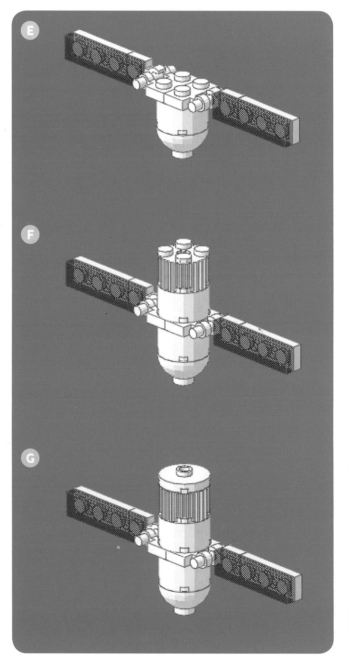

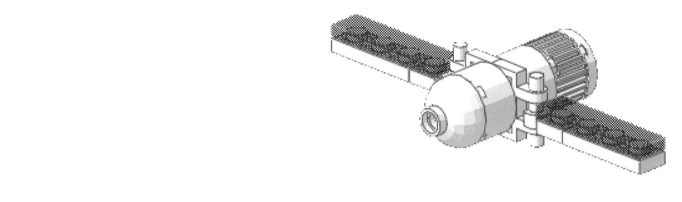

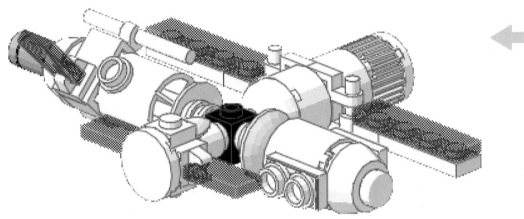

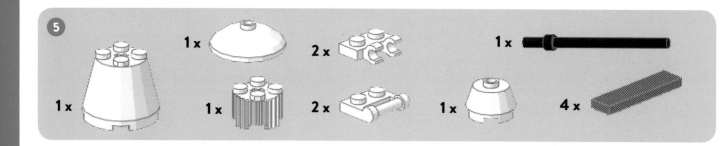

5

1 x   1 x   2 x   1 x

1 x   2 x   1 x   4 x

A

B

C

D

E

F

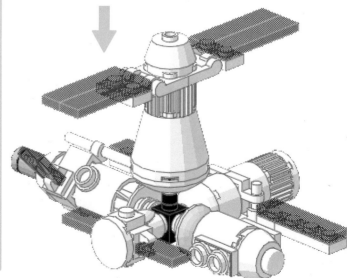

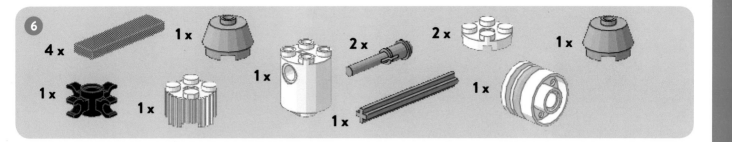

6 4 x   1 x   2 x   2 x   1 x   1 x   1 x   1 x

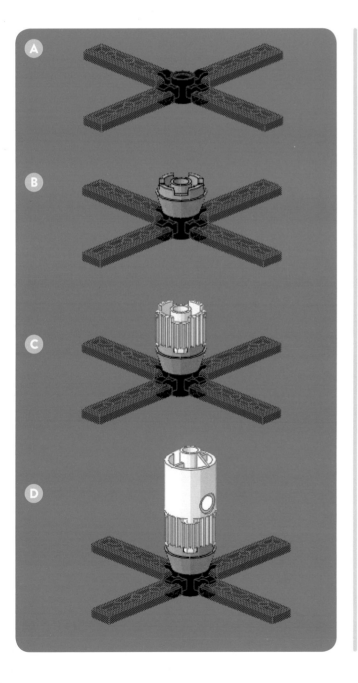

A

B

C

D

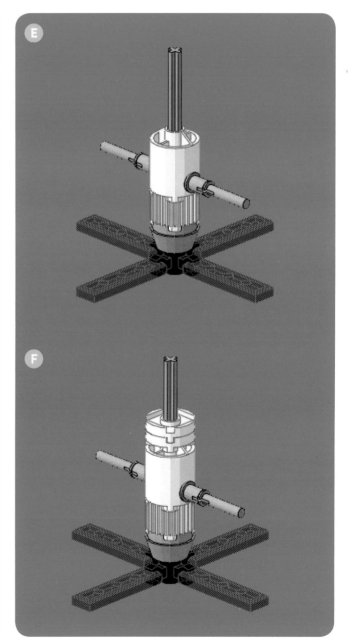

E

F

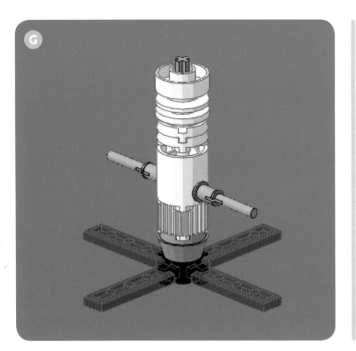

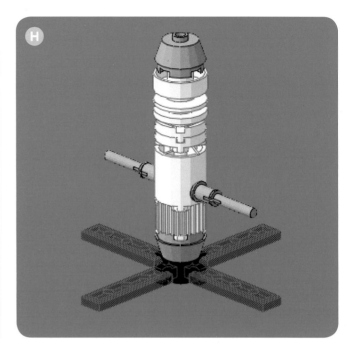

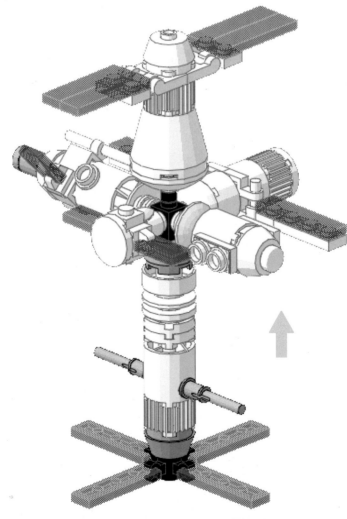

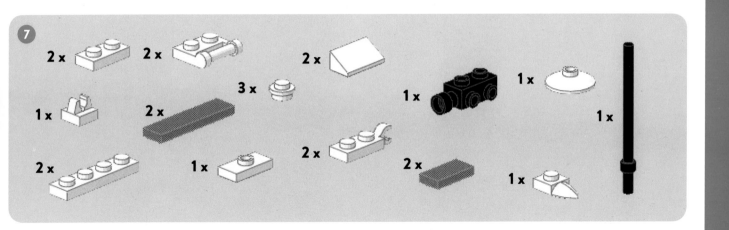

7

2 x · 2 x · 2 x · 1 x · 1 x

1 x · 2 x · 3 x · 1 x · 1 x

2 x · 1 x · 2 x · 2 x · 1 x

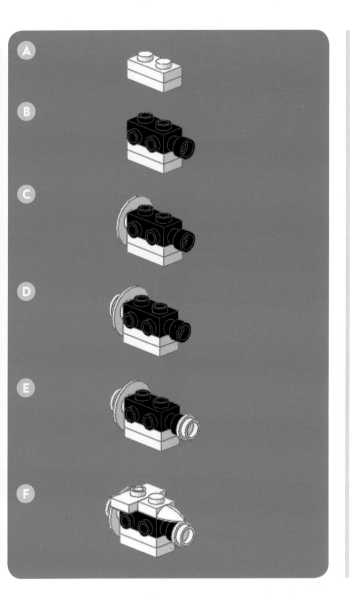

A
B
C
D
E
F

G

H

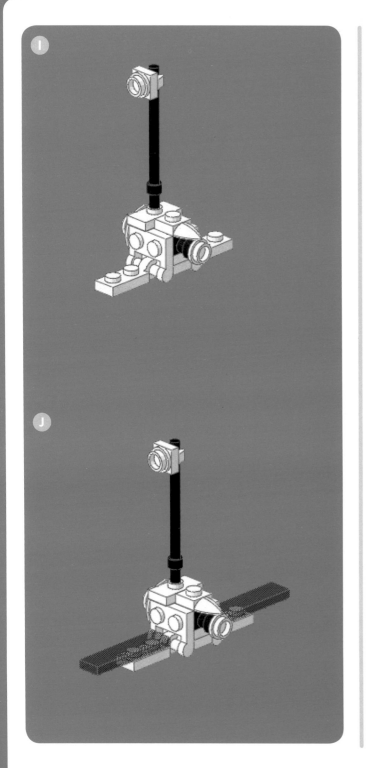

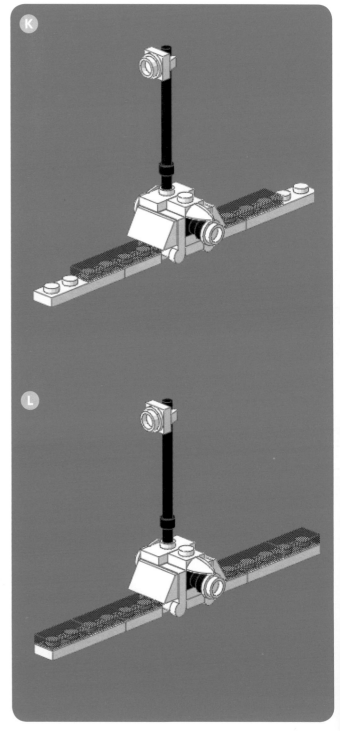

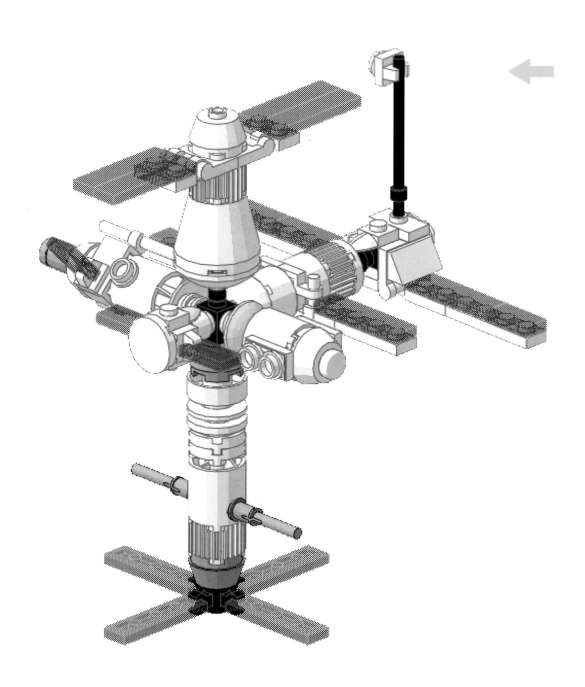

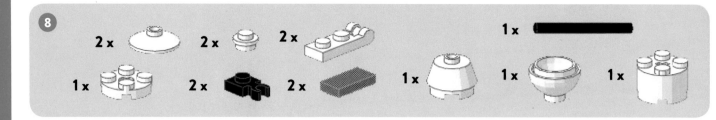

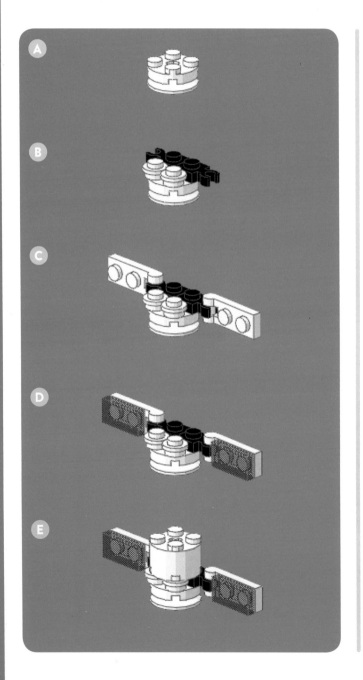

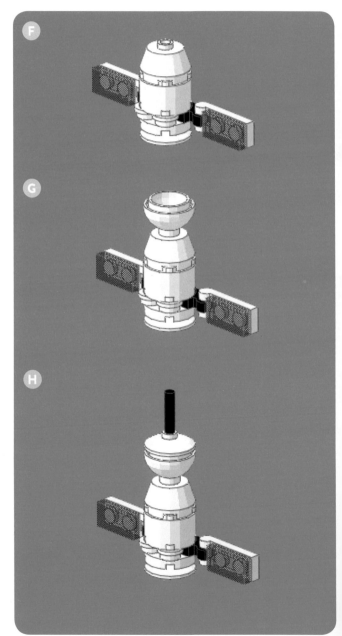

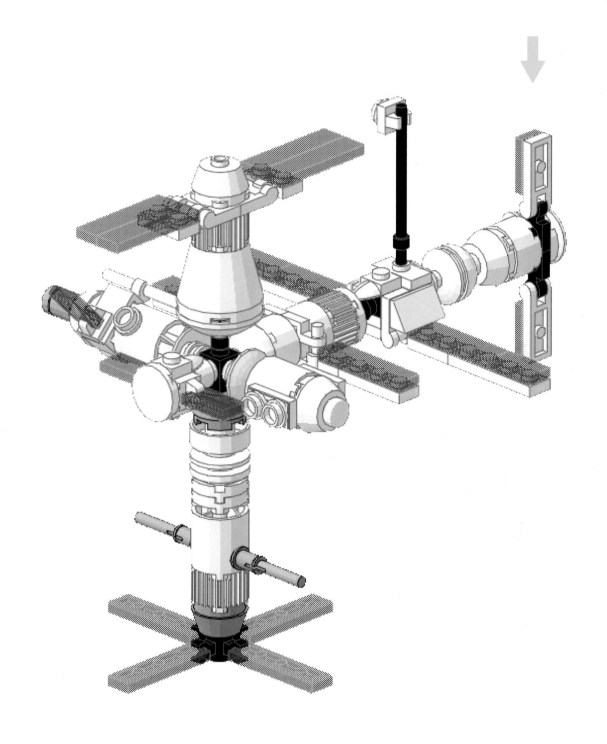

ASTRONAUTS

Astronauts are people who are trained to command or pilot a spacecraft, or to work on board a space station. In Russia, astronauts are called cosmonauts. The first human in space was cosmonaut Yuri Gagarin (1934–1968), who orbited the Earth for 108 minutes in the Soviet Union's Vostok 1 spacecraft in 1961.

TRAINING

Before they are selected to take part in a mission, astronauts who are commanders and pilots usually have many years of experience as pilots of jet aircraft. Astronauts who will carry out research on the International Space Station (ISS) may be scientists or mathematicians. Sometimes teachers are chosen for the ISS. They broadcast experiments to children back on Earth.

All astronauts and cosmonauts go through at least 20 months of training. They are trained in piloting craft and doing spacewalks. Spacewalks are usually performed while tethered, or tied, to a spacecraft. Occasionally, they are untethered, if the astronaut is using a propulsion unit, which flies using its own tank of fuel. Trainees also experience near weightlessness on board a high-speed aircraft. Astronauts call this the "vomit comet".

NASA astronaut Mike Fossum trains while completing a mission in the custom version of his spacesuit.

Mission specialist Carlos I. Noriega waves at his spacewalk partner, Joseph R. Tanner, outside the ISS in December 2000.

SPACESUITS

While inside a pressurized space station, where the temperature is comfortable and the air is right for breathing, astronauts wear ordinary, loose clothes. They need to bring lots of extra underwear, because there is no washing machine. For flights to and from Earth, astronauts put on Launch and Entry Suits, which include a parachute and would protect them from loss of air pressure.

For spacewalks, astronauts wear a spacesuit. These protect astronauts from the dangers of space. They are strong enough to keep out space radiation and space dust. A helmet, breathing apparatus, and oxygen tank allow astronauts to breathe in the vacuum of space. Spacesuits also keep astronauts at the right temperature, as space is very cold in the shade and extremely hot in the sunlight. There is also a water supply in case an astronaut gets thirsty.

An astronaut strapped into his bunk in the ISS sleeping quarters. Sleeping in space can be hard for astronauts to adjust to. They have to be strapped in so that they don't float around and bump into things!

ASTRONAUT

An astronaut can be up to 5 cm (2 in) taller after coming back from space. The cartilage discs in the spine expand because of the lack of gravity.

PIECES REQUIRED

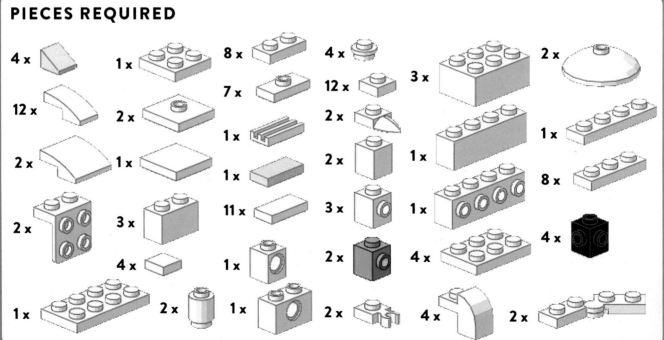

4 x   1 x   8 x   4 x   3 x   2 x

12 x   2 x   7 x   12 x   1 x

2 x   1 x   1 x   2 x   1 x   8 x

2 x   3 x   11 x   1 x   3 x   1 x   4 x

4 x   1 x   2 x   4 x

1 x   2 x   1 x   2 x   4 x   2 x

1
2 x
1 x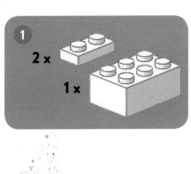

2
1 x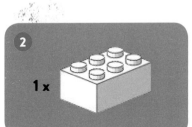

3
3 x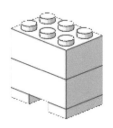

4
1 x  2 x

5
1 x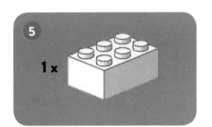

6
1 x 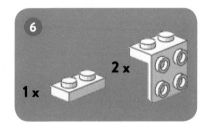 2 x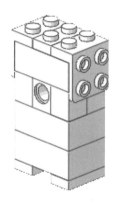

7
2 x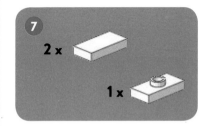
1 x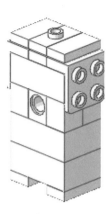

8
2 x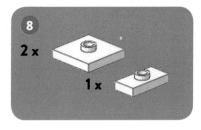
1 x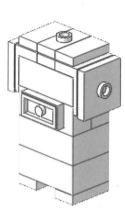

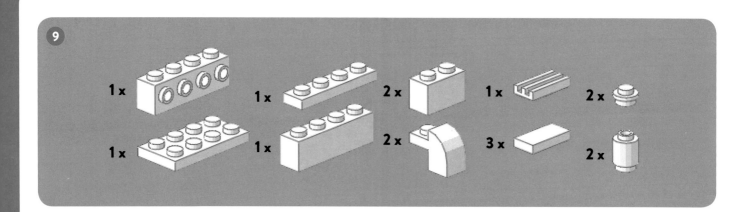

1 x   1 x   2 x   1 x   2 x

1 x   1 x   2 x   3 x   2 x

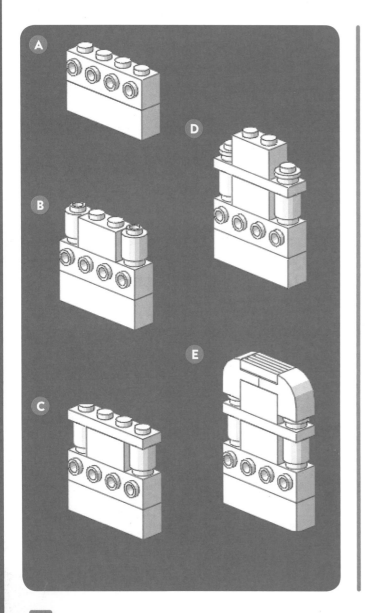

A

B

C

D

E

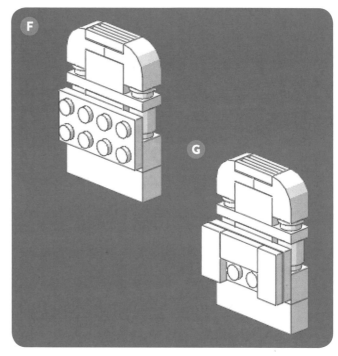

F

G

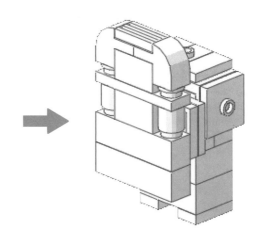

10

1x 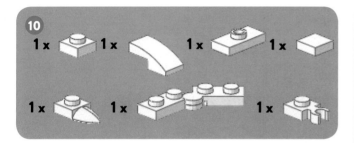 1x   1x   1x

1x   1x   1x

A

B

11

1x   1x   1x   1x

1x   1x   1x

A

B

12

2x   2x   1x

1x   1x   1x

2x   2x   4x

A   E

B   F

C   G

D

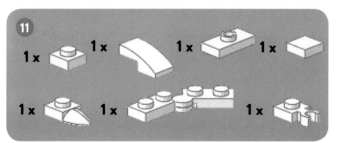
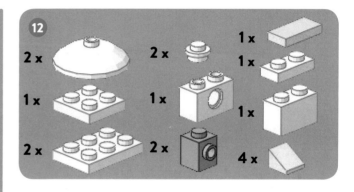
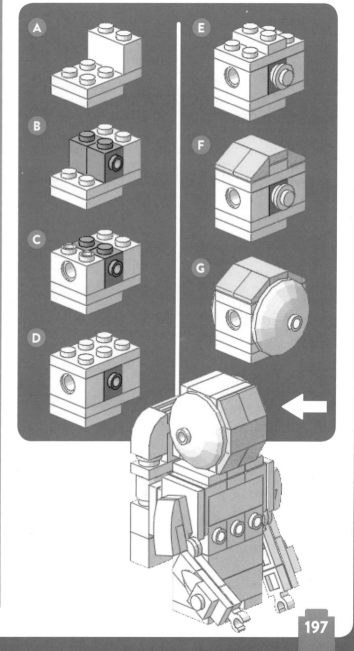

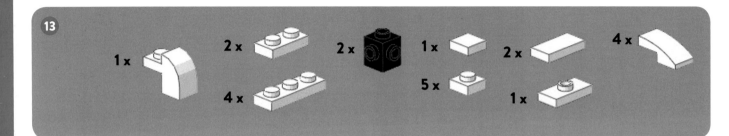

13

1 x   2 x   4 x   2 x   1 x   5 x   2 x   1 x   4 x

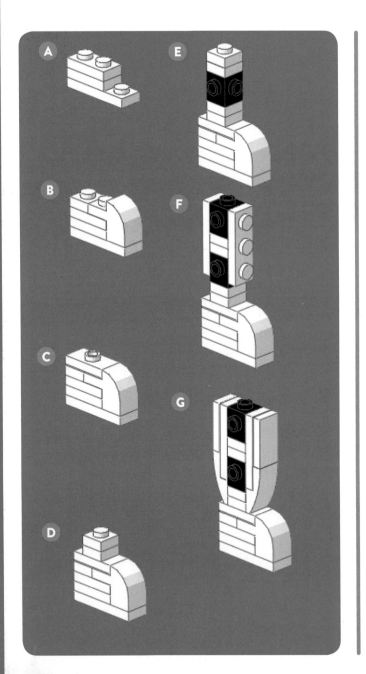

A

B

C

D

E

F

G

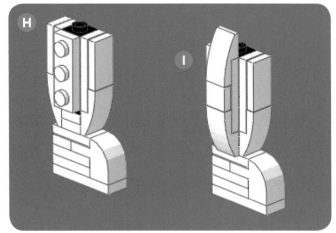

H

I

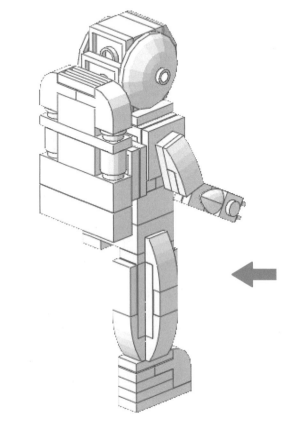

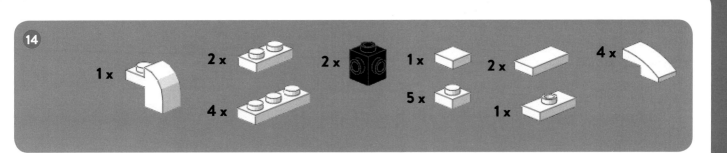

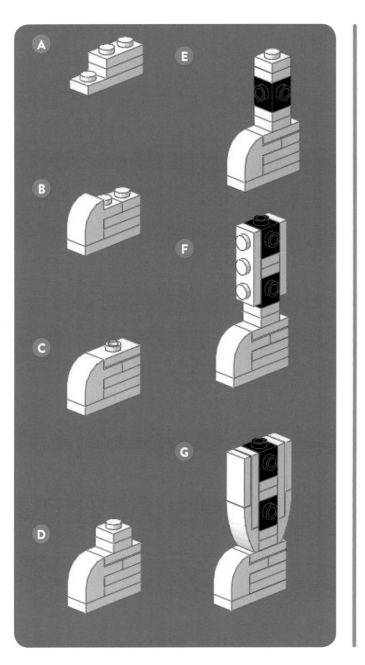

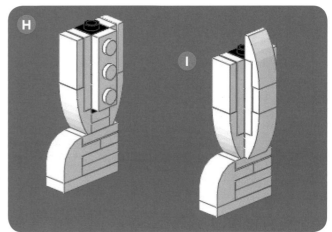

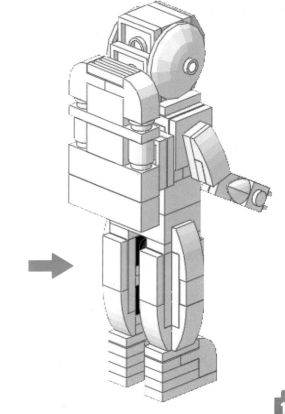

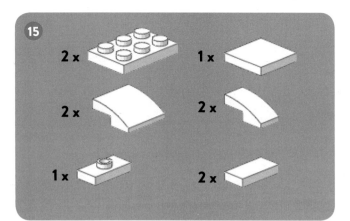

15

2 x   1 x

2 x   2 x

1 x   2 x

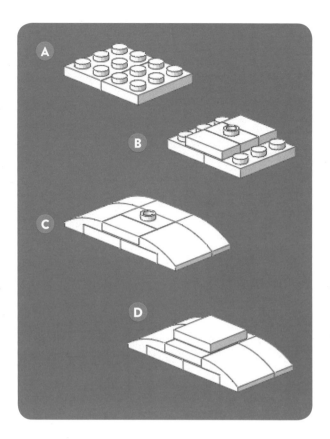

A

B

C

D

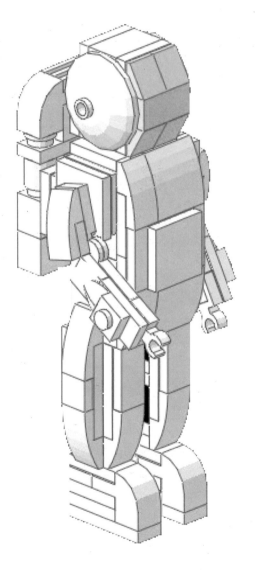

FACT

- It's not only humans that fly into space. Laika, a stray dog chosen by the Russian space agency, became the first living thing to go into space in 1957.

CIVILIAN TRAVEL

Most people who travel into space are professional astronauts who are trained and paid by their government's space agency. However, a few people have been lucky enough to visit space by paying for the trip themselves. These civilian astronauts are sometimes called space tourists.

SPACE STATION VISITS

The first civilian astronaut was a US businessman called Dennis Tito (born 1940). In 2001, he paid around $20 million to spend seven days on the International Space Station. Before setting off on a Russian Soyuz spacecraft, he trained alongside professional astronauts for many months. It is extremely expensive for governments to keep the ISS in orbit, so a handful of other paying visitors have been allowed to join the international crew since Tito's visit.

One day, it will probably be possible to stay in a space hotel in orbit around the Earth. Businesses such as Bigelow Aerospace and the Space Island Group are planning to create space stations that will offer accommodation for hundreds or even thousands of people. These hotels might offer "zero-gravity" sports and space-walks.

Dennis Tito with cosmonauts Talgat Musabayev and Yury Baturin on their way to the ISS. (left to right)

The Virgin Galactic reusable, sub-orbital spacecraft on display at an airshow.

SUB-ORBITAL FLIGHTS

Staying in a space station in Earth orbit is too expensive for everyone except billionaires, but several businesses are planning to offer cheaper sub-orbital space flights. Sub-orbital flights enter space but are too low to go into orbit around Earth. For a cost of around $200,000, passengers will reach heights of up to 160 km (100 miles) above Earth and experience a feeling of weightlessness for several minutes.

Sir Richard Branson's Virgin Galactic company plans to offer sub-orbital flights on a fleet of five SpaceShipTwo space planes. These will be lifted to a height of 16 km (10 miles) by WhiteKnightTwo jet-powered cargo planes, then released to complete the flight. Unlike SpaceShipTwo, the Lynx sub-orbital vehicle will not need a mothership to lift it into the air. It will take off from a runway under its own rocket power, but will have room for only a pilot and one space tourist.

Professor Stephen Hawking on a zero gravity flight. These flights are a great way for non-astronauts to experience weightlessness without leaving Earth's orbit!

WHITEKNIGHTTWO

The WhiteKnightTwo's first flight was in 2008. It was designed for multiple uses, including training people in zero-gravity, science experiments in micro-gravity and to launch other payloads into space.

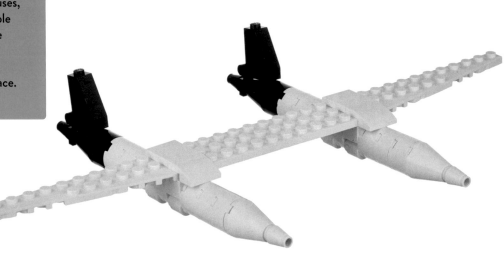

PIECES REQUIRED

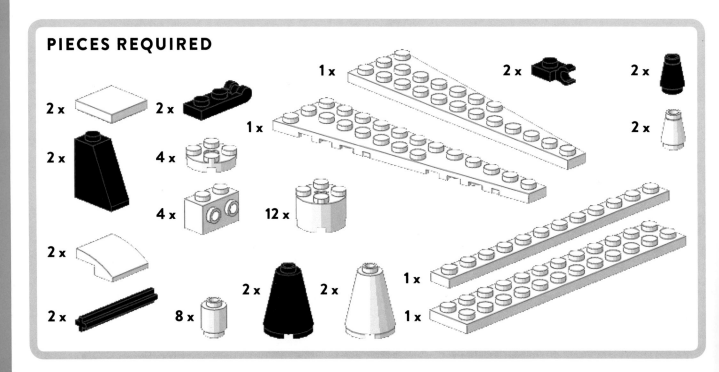

2 x   2 x   1 x   2 x   2 x

2 x   4 x   1 x   2 x

2 x   4 x   12 x

2 x

2 x   8 x   2 x   2 x   1 x

1 x

1

3 x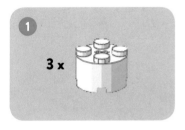

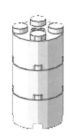

2

2 x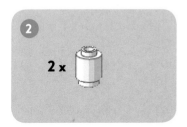

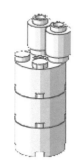

3

1 x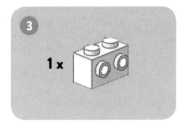

4

2 x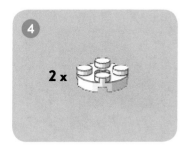

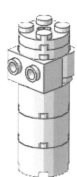

5

2 x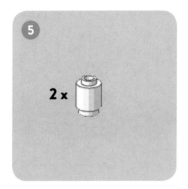

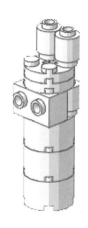

6

1 x

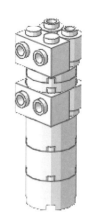

7

3 x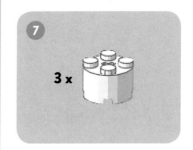

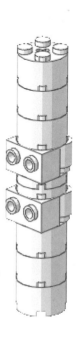

8

1x

1x

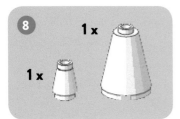

9

1x

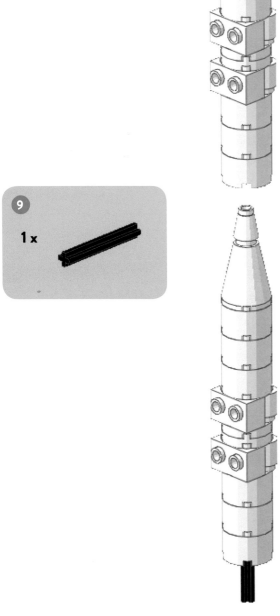

10

1x 1x 1x

1x 1x

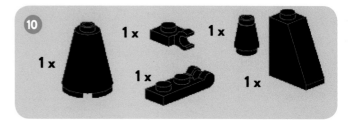

A

B

C

D

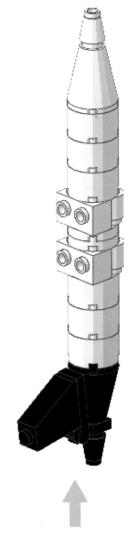

make
2

11

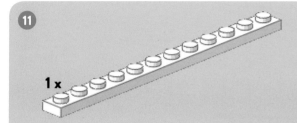

1 x

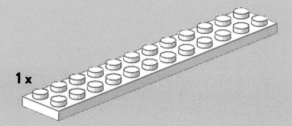

1 x

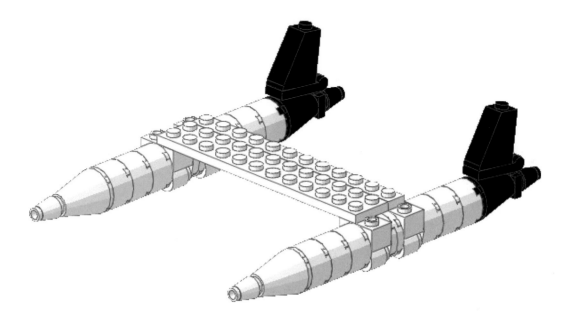

FACT

- WhiteKnightTwo is designed to lift the SpaceShipTwo spaceplane to a height of 15 km (50,000 ft), where it releases its cargo and returns to Earth. It first flew in December 2008.

- With a wingspan of 43 metres (141 ft), WhiteKnightTwo has four jet engines and twin fuselages. Its two pilots sit in the right-hand fuselage.

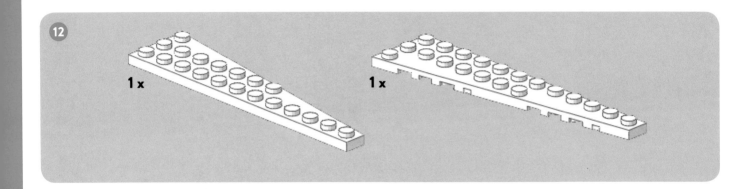

1x   1x

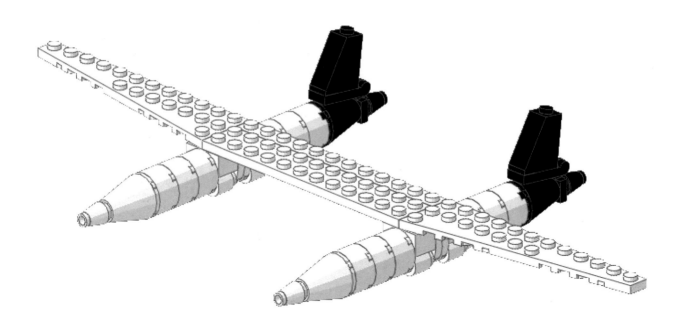

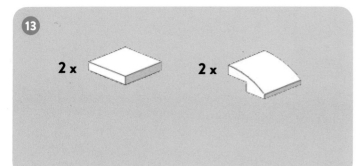

13

2 x   2 x

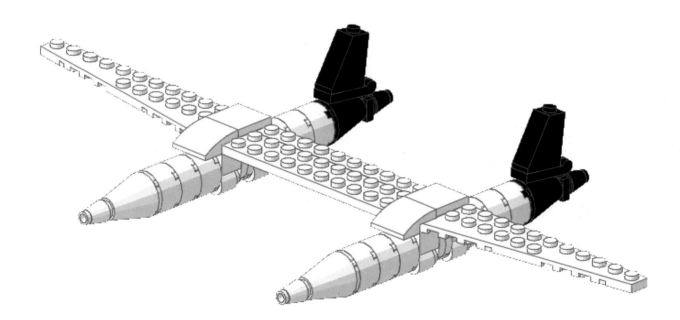

SPACESHIPTWO

SpaceShipTwo is a spaceplane designed for space tourism. Its first powered flight was in 2013. It gets carried to altitude by the WhiteKnightTwo.

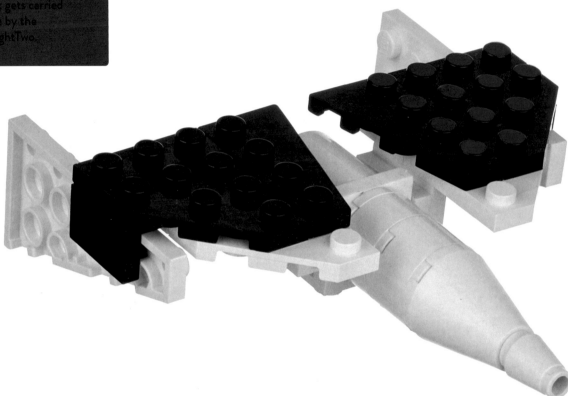

 Once you've built both the WhiteKnightTwo and the SpaceShipTwo, you can fit them together with just one 1x1 white brick. Add it to the top of the SpaceShipTwo, and off you go!

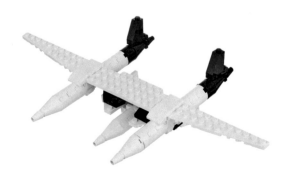

PIECES REQUIRED

1 x

1 x

2 x

1 x

1 x

2 x

2 x

2 x

1 x

2 x

2 x

2 x

1 x

2 x

1 x

1 x

1 x

1 x

1 x

1

1 x   1 x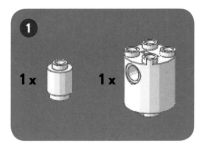

2

1 x   1 x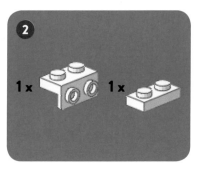

3

1 x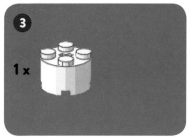

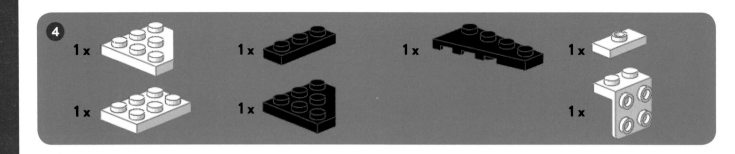

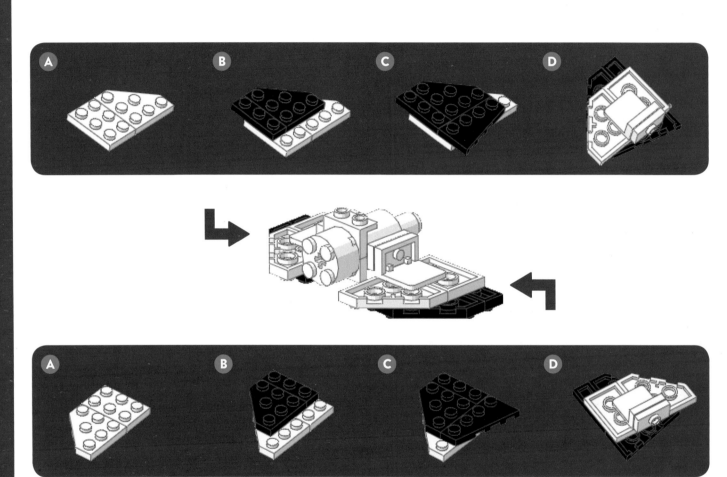

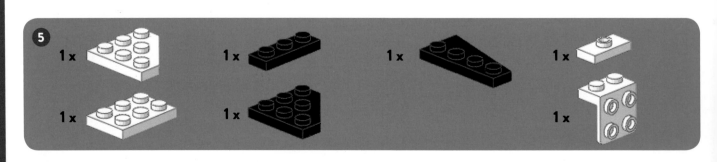

6

1 x 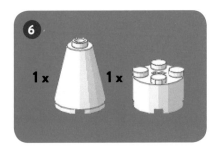 1 x

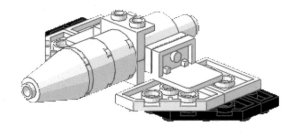

7

2 x 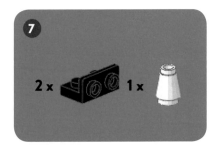 1 x

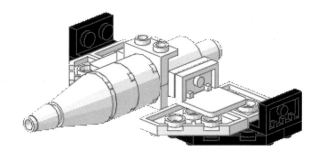

8

1 x

1 x

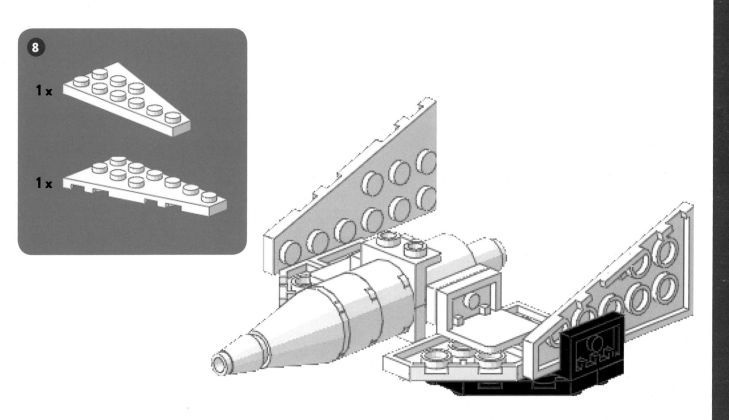

THE FUTURE

We have come a long way since the Soviet Union sent the first satellite, Sputnik 1, into space in 1957. We have landed humans on the Moon, used rovers to investigate Mars, and sent probes beyond our Solar System. What are the next challenges for space exploration?

Astronaut Charles Conrad Jr., commander of the Apollo 12 mission to the moon.

TO THE MOON...

Apart from Earth, the Moon is the only object in the Solar System on which humans have set foot. We have not walked there since 1972. NASA, as well as the Chinese, European, Indian, and Russian space agencies, is planning to send astronauts back to the Moon. The next step would be to build a permanent Moon base where astronauts could live and work.

On the Moon, astronauts could develop the skills and technology needed to explore more distant worlds. They could also experiment with making supplies of rocket fuel and oxygen, using materials found on the Moon. The Moon may one day become a refueling stop-off, or a base for launching more distant missions.

Concept art created by NASA shows astronauts entering a lunar outpost.

Mars Curiosity Rover testing the soil on Mars. The information it uncovers may help future settlers.

AND BEYOND...

NASA has plans to send astronauts to an asteroid by 2025, and to Mars by the 2030s. To do that, we need to develop larger spacecraft to accommodate crew on a six-month journey, as well as more powerful rockets to launch them. NASA is currently testing the Orion Multi-Purpose Crew Vehicle, which could carry a crew of four. It is hoped it will carry its first astronauts in 2023.

The astronaut Buzz Aldrin, who walked on the Moon in 1969, has proposed a one-way mission to Mars, where volunteers would build a permanent settlement. Over time, workers might undertake the terra-forming of Mars. "Terra-forming" means turning another planet into an Earth-like environment. This might be done by artificially raising Mars's temperature and using chemistry to release water and breathable gases from the rock. The technology to do this still needs to be invented, but scientists believe it might just be possible.

GLOSSARY

Asteroid
A stony and/or metallic object less than 1000-km (600-miles) wide that orbits the Sun.

Asteroid belt
A group of asteroids orbiting the Sun in the space between the orbits of Mars and Jupiter.

Astronaut
A person who goes into outer space (called cosmonauts in Russia).

Atmosphere
A layer of gases attached to a planet or moon by gravity.

Big Bang
The theoretical creation of the universe about 13.8 billion years ago.

Cosmonaut
The Russian name for an astronaut (a person who goes into outer space).

Dwarf planet
An object orbiting the sun that is not quite spherical or has multiple pieces. Pluto is a dwarf planet.

Galileo Galilei
An Italian astronomer born in 1564 and called "the father of observational astronomy".

Galaxy
A group of stars, gas, and dust held together by gravity.

Gas Giant
A giant planet made of of mostly hydrogen and helium. In the Solar System this includes Saturn and Jupiter.

Ice giant
A giant planet made up of heavy elements like oxygen, carbon, nitrogen, and sulfur. In the Solar System this includes Uranus and Neptune.

Milky Way
The galaxy that the Solar System is a part of. It looks like a glowing stripe in the sky from Earth.

Orbit
The regular, repeating path of an object in space around a larger object. The object in orbit is called a satellite. The Earth is a natural satellite of the Sun, and many robotic satellites circle the Earth.

Orbital module
The part of a spacecraft that is only used once in orbit.

Plasma
A building block of the universe, similar to gas.

Probes
A robotic spacecraft that explores space.

Re-entry module
The part of a spacecraft that returns to Earth.

Rocket
A type of engine that can work in space, where there is no air. The word "rocket" can also mean a ship that uses this type of engine.

Satellite
Any object in space that orbits another object is called a satellite, but the word usually means a machine that has been launched into space to orbit the Earth.

Service module
The part of a spacecraft that holds the rocket engine.

Space Station
A habitable human-made satellite that orbits Earth conducting research.

Spacesuit
More than just clothes astronauts wear in space, a spacesuit is more like a small spacecraft. It holds air to breathe and water to drink, and keeps astronauts safe from all the dangers of space.

Terra-forming
The idea of changing a planet to be more like the Earth, and able to support human life.

Terrestrial planet
A planet made up of mostly rocks and metals. In the Solar System this includes Earth, Mercury, Venus, and Mars.

INDEX

ABOUT THE AUTHOR

DO YOU REALLY BUILD LEGO® MODELS FOR A LIVING?

It's a question I'm asked again and again and the answer is "yes". I really do build LEGO® models for a living and it's a pretty good job! I think what people really would like to know, though, is how I ended up with this job and what we really do, day-in and day-out. So, this is the story!

As a child I was always interested in LEGO® sets. Each January I would get hold of the latest catalogue and look at all the new sets that were going to be released that year. I'd decide which ones I'd ask my parents for on my birthday – and which sets I'd ask Father Christmas if he could find for me. Usually I was very lucky and I built up a huge LEGO® collection. Like most children at that time though, come the age of 15 or 16 I put my LEGO® aside and became more interested in other things!

I came back to LEGO® as in my mid twenties. In 2000, The LEGO® Group released a Statue of Liberty model and again, I was bought a LEGO® set as a gift. That set kicked my interest back into action and I quickly became an "Adult Fan of LEGO®". As an AFOL I built models of things that I knew and eventually I started being asked to build models for other people. In 2012, I was lucky enough to be asked by Visit Denmark (the Danish tourist board) and LEGO® themselves to build something to commemorate the London Olympics. At the same time I was in the middle of writing my very first book and quickly I had more LEGO® "work" than real work. So I took the plunge!

Since I started building LEGO® models full time, things have grown very rapidly. My company now has four employees (including myself) and we operate from a small studio just outside of Edinburgh, Scotland. Sadly, we don't get to build something every day but when we do our studio is organized perfectly to let us build whatever we need. In the centre of our building space is a large table. A very large table! It seems that whatever we build from LEGO® needs lots and lots of space.

Lining our studio down the two long walls are racks and racks of drawers. So that we can build anything, we try to keep a very good stock of pieces available. Along one side of the studio are the basics – bricks, plates, and tiles. Down the other side are all the "specials". Slopes, rounds, parts with bars, parts with clips – they are all here. Each draw is then subdivided with small tubs. So a draw of 2x2 round plates might have drawers of red, white, blue, yellow parts, etc.

We keep about 4 million elements in stock at any one time and everything has its place! We've found that being ultra-organized has doubled the speed at which we can build models, which is handy when you have more than 30 models to build for one book!

Whilst sometimes we have the liberty of choosing what to build, or how to build it, there are times when our models have to be extremely precise. If this is the case, then often we don't start with LEGO® bricks at all. The first stage is on computer. Building digitally lets me work on a design that might be too large to test in real life, too complex – or just far too fiddly! Using a specific LEGO® computer aided design package, I can create models that don't have to worry about gravity just yet. We can then work on these until it's finally time to work out how to put those bricks together so they do actually fit!

So it's true, I do get paid to build LEGO® models for a living and it is my dream job. I will just sound a word of warning though – it doesn't mean that you don't have to go to school or get any qualifications! Just like any career, to do my job you need a good selection of skills. Not only do I have to build with LEGO® but I also need to be able to use 3-D CAD programs, make calculations about size and volume, write business proposals, and even balance the books! A good basis in maths, geometry, IT, and English are all essential skills. Art and Design helps too, though I'll admit I am terrible with a pencil!

CREDITS

Warren Elsmore is an artist in LEGO® bricks and a lifelong fan of LEGO® who is based in Edinburgh, U.K. He has been in love with the little plastic bricks since the age of four and now spends his days creating amazing models out of LEGO® bricks.

After 15 years in a successful IT career, in 2012 Warren moved to working full time with LEGO® bricks . He now helps companies such as IBM, LEGO®, DFDS, WPP and VisitDenmark© to realize their own dreams in plastic. Warren's bestselling first book (*Brick City*) was released in 21 languages to critical acclaim and has been followed by a range of books each recreating parts of the world we inhabit in plastic bricks. His models have always attracted great press coverage – one of his models has even made it as far as the South Pole thanks to the British Antarctic Survey!

Exhibitions of three of Warren's books (*Brick City*, *Wonders*, and *History*) tour museums and galleries throughout Europe, entertaining hundreds of thousands of children of all ages. In 2014, Warren co-launched "BRICK" – the largest LEGO® fan event in the UK and one of the largest in the world.

For more information, please visit warrenelsmore.com.

Brick photography by Neal Grundy.

Space text written by Fay Evans and Claudia Martin.

Weldon Owen would like to thank Warren Elsmore, Neal Grundy, Rhys Knight, Claudia Martin, and all the contributors for their stellar input.

PICTURE CREDITS